Key Persons in the Early Years

Key Persons in the Early Years aims to explain what a Key Person is, the theory behind the approach and the practicalities of implementation. Practical in its approach and containing case studies as examples of reflective practice, this second edition details the role of the Key Person across all ages in the early years. This new edition has been fully updated in line with the Early Years Foundation Stage and features a new chapter on the Key Persons approach with 3- to 5-year-olds.

The book offers guidance on:

- making the Key Persons approach work in your setting, with realistic strategies;
- the benefits of this approach for children's well-being, for their learning and to ensure equal chances for all children;
- potential challenges and problems and how to overcome them, drawing on accounts from practitioners of their journey in implementing this approach.

This book will be an essential text for practitioners and students who wish to fully understand the Key Persons role and how it can benefit children, parents and their setting.

Peter Elfer is Senior Lecturer in Early Childhood Studies at Roehampton University.

Elinor Goldschmied was an internationally renowned trainer and early years consultant and her work continues to have a profound influence on theory and practice today. She is best known for introducing the Treasure Basket, Heuristic Play with objects and the Key Persons approach into early years practice.

Dorothy Y. Selleck is an independent early years consultant working in local authorities around the UK, leading training and mentoring for schools and settings on the Key Persons approach.

Key Persons in the Early Years

Building relationships for quality provision in early years settings and primary schools

Second edition

Peter Elfer, Elinor Goldschmied and Dorothy Y. Selleck

Routledge
Taylor & Francis Group

LONDON AND NEW YORK

First edition published 2005
as *Key Persons in the Nursery*
by David Fulton Publishers

This second edition published 2012
by Routledge
2 Park Square, Milton Park, Abingdon, Oxon OX14 4RN

Simultaneously published in the USA and Canada
by Routledge
711 Third Avenue, New York, NY 10017

Routledge is an imprint of the Taylor & Francis Group, an informa business

© 2012 Peter Elfer, Elinor Goldschmied and Dorothy Y. Selleck

British Library Cataloguing in Publication Data
A catalogue record for this book is available from the British Library

Library of Congress Cataloging in Publication Data
Elfer, Peter.
Key persons in the early years : building relationships for quality provision in early years
settings and primary schools / by Peter Elfer, Elinor Goldschmied, and Dorothy Y. Selleck.
— 2nd editon.
p. cm.
Includes bibliographical references and index.
1. Elementary school teaching. 2. Effective teaching. 3. Elementary school teachers—
Professional relationships. I. Goldschmied, Elinor. II. Selleck, Dorothy Y. III. Title.
LB1555.E444 2012
372.1102—dc22
2011012253

ISBN: 978-0-415-61038-4 (hbk)
ISBN: 978-0-415-61039-1 (pbk)
ISBN: 978-0-203-80471-1 (ebk)

Typeset in Bembo
by FiSH Books

Printed and bound in Great Britain by
IJ International Ltd, Padstow, Cornwall

Contents

Figures and tables

Tables

Preface

Children begin their lives with us in the safe places of laps, homes and early childhood centres, and in the places we walk, talk and travel as families and communities. However loved and cherished children may be, childhood includes times and events that may be difficult or painful for children. Ordinary childhoods and ordinary growing up, alongside the magical, loving, enchanting times, also are times of difficult emotions, sadness, fear, anxiety, perhaps occasionally even terror, loss and bereavement.

Toddlers who are 'up' and wide eyed and whirring like aeroplanes above an adult's shoulders, and 'down' to terrible crashes on soft sofas, are rehearsing triumphs and treacheries. This 'playing up' and 'playing it out' is the stuff of growing up. Powerful thinkers, lovers and learners begin in families, and often go on to early years centres to live and learn these things too.

We think that what babies and young children experience in the beginning makes a difference, in families but also in early years centres. Adults at home help children manage the emotional roller coaster that life can be. Parents do this for their children as part of the day to day job of parenting, even if some of the time the incessant demands of children growing up can threaten to overwhelm most parents. The paradox of parenting is that it is so ordinary and so special at the same time.

In *Key Persons in the Early Years* we argue that the youngest children also need special kinds of relationships to set them up right when they are cared for away from their parents. Children from different families have very different experiences (for example playing in private gardens, travelling the hills and dales in the family van, watching videos, being carried through markets or sitting on the end of the supermarket trolley).

One or two practitioners in the setting, whilst never taking over from parents, need to connect with what parents would ordinarily do. That is, they need to be special for each child; help them manage throughout the day, think about them, get to know them well, and sometimes worry about them too, so as to help them to make a strong link between home and setting. We have called the two people that carry that role for a child, the child's *Key Persons*. The strategy that makes it all happen is the *Key Persons approach*.

Peter Elfer, Elinor Goldschmied and Dorothy Y. Selleck

Postcript for this second edition

Elinor died in 2009 and we are sad that she has not been able to contribute to this second edition of the book. We remain in active contact with many of the practitioners, trainers, academics and friends of hers, here in the UK as well as in Italy. We share a sense of gratitude for her huge legacy of the sense of how much it mattered to babies and young children to have someone in their early years setting for whom they are special. Elinor used to speak of the child 'being camped out, as it were, in the adult's mind'. Part of this legacy was also Elinor's commitment, without ever compromising the principle of 'professional' attachments, to continually explore and learn about how such attachments can work in the most respectful and effective way for all involved. We hope you the reader will join us in continuing that journey of research, exploration and understanding.

Peter Elfer and Dorothy Y. Selleck

Acknowledgements

The inspiration for the Key Persons approach came from the international work of Elinor Goldschmied, a trainer and consultant on good practice in nurseries.

Our evolving understanding over the years of the three authors thinking together about the subtleties of the interactions between parents, children and staff in early years settings and schools would never have got off the starting blocks if many early years managers and staff had not been so open to us spending time in their settings observing what went on.

We want to pay tribute to the professional openness and generosity of many parents and practitioners, friends and colleagues, who often seemed to be speaking to us very much from the heart. But it is the babies and young children who, when we found ways to listen carefully enough, taught us most about what matters in nurseries, often long before they could talk.

CHAPTER

1

Parenting and working, children and settings
Achieving life balances

Public policy and private choices

> Are work and family life compatible? All too often parents find it impossible to
> balance employment and care commitments. Reconciling work and family life is
> important to individuals and societies. Parents who wish to care for their children
> by giving up work should have their choice respected. Often, however, this
> 'choice' is constrained, because parents see no way of giving their children the care
> and education they need at the same time as working in today's demanding labour
> market. Yet children whose parents are not in paid work are likely to be poor,
> while mothers who have interrupted their careers to care for their children are at
> higher risk of poverty when they are older. The ability to generate income in a
> fulfilling job and the desire to provide the best for one's children, giving them the
> care and nurturing they need, do not have to be mutually exclusive.
>
> (OECD, 2005)

The practicalities for parents of finding a job and an early years place for the children
where the hours fit together, never mind the journeys, is not at all straightforward. If
parents also have children of school age, the logistics are worse. Then there are holidays, late starts on days following holidays and INSET days. Covering for when
children are unwell can barely be thought about.

But achieving a balance of family life and work, connecting the worlds of home
and the early years setting is much more than the fitting of work round setting hours
or setting round working hours, as difficult as that is. There are emotional transactions
to be negotiated: balancing personal needs and children's needs, time at home and
earning an income for the family, being a 'good' employee but also being a 'good'
parent. Although parents are very different from one another and have different
approaches to bringing up their children, almost all parents want the very best for
their child. Compromises are always necessary in life, but for most parents their children matter more than anything else. Striking these balances has to be done in a

society that seems to be continually changing its policies and attitudes to earning and parenting. Public policy has certainly come a long way in the last 60 years.

While recent governments have wanted to encourage both women and men to work outside the home, this has certainly not always been the approach. At the close of World War II, the Ministry of Health could not have been more explicit:

> in the interests of the health and development of the child … the right policy to pursue would be positively to discourage mothers of children under two from going out to work.
>
> (Ministry of Health and Ministry of Education, 1945: 1)

Since 1945, the demand for greater fairness between women and men, equality of opportunity, changing family needs and the growth of the economy have combined to gradually enable a change of message from Government about how our youngest children are cared for.

In the years since 1945, the attitudes of government towards child care, evident in the circular quoted above with its message that women with children under the age of 2 should not work, have changed completely. Governments since 1994 have achieved a lot:

> The authors of this paper are not alone in applauding the government's achievements. Tremendous progress has been made in children's services in England since the first OECD review took place in December 1999. Most noteworthy are the significant increase in investment, the expansion of (local) Sure Start schemes and new moves towards children's centres and extended schools.
>
> (private communication from John Bennett, author of the OECD report on early years, 2004, quoted in Pugh and Sylva 2005: 22)

An aspect of this 'tremendous progress' has been the increasing attention successive governments have given to the Key Person role and its importance. In the guidance issued with the Children Act 1989 (Department of Health, 1991), the importance to children's well-being of consistent individual attention from a practitioner who knew that child well was emphasised. That value of each child having his own Key Person was a guiding principle of the *Birth to Three Matters* framework issued by the Government in 2002 (DfES, 2002). Another big step forward was made with the introduction of *The Early Years Foundation Stage* in September 2008, when the Key Persons role was made a duty ('you must') rather than just a recommendation ('it would be a good idea if…') (DfES, 2007).

Yet even back in 2005, Gillian Pugh and Kathy Sylva did not wear rose-tinted spectacles. They described a number of serious challenges still to be faced to develop a genuinely child-centred, integrated, accessible service working closely in partnership with parents. Further, as we write, the news is dominated by the imposition of spending cuts by the Coalition Government and the intention to move away from the aim of universal provision for all children and back to targeted provision for children and families considered to be most in need. The Early Years Foundation

Stage is being reviewed by Dame Claire Tickell and it is likely that we will see some considerable changes to it.

So public policy and the legislation, duties and guidance that accompany it, impacts directly on the private choices parents make because it influences the very supply of early years places, their cost and their quality in general and very specific ways. We know from professional experience, research evidence and from having children and grandchildren of our own, just how much it matters what each early years setting is like. We know too how much difference it makes to know that there is someone in the early years setting who has special responsibility for each child and for helping that child build a special bond of belonging.

As well as public policy, public attitudes impact on private choices too. The roles women and men, mothers and fathers take at home and at work, as portrayed on the television and film, in newspapers and magazines, also shape the life balances that families strike. At one time it was seen as irresponsible if a father did not work outside the home but irresponsible if a mother did. An opposite but equally powerful theme suggested women were bored or boring if they did not work outside the home. Many mothers seemed to feel blamed and shamed whatever they did.

For many parents, particularly mothers, there still seems to be quite a deep anxiety about whether the care of children outside the family home, however good it is, can be good enough. Yet the main conclusion of researchers is that good quality services are not harmful and may bring many benefits (Melhuish, 2004; Belsky *et al.,* 2007; NICHD, 1997). At home, they allow both parents to work and have a better standard of living. And children may end up with the best of both worlds, the love and uniqueness of private family life but also the advantage of being part of a public community of adults and other children in the early years setting.

Alongside changes in public policy, more flexibility and less blame in cultural attitudes about the roles men and women actually take has seemed to free up the private choices that can be made about how child rearing, earning a living and running a home can be shared.

How 'free' such choices feel to those who make them and how well they work out in practice depends on many factors and not least levels of wages parents receive and levels of charges for early years places they have to pay. The flexibility of working hours and the hours of the early years setting are key factors too. Alongside these essential practicalities, we believe there are two other critical factors that determine the impact of early years care and education on the daily lives of children, parents, and practitioners: first, the quality of the early years setting; and second, how the two worlds of home and setting are enabled to join up. We believe the key to both these factors converges in the idea of the Key Persons approach. The remainder of Chapter 1 is devoted to saying why.

What counts in quality?

'Quality' is a slippery idea. It is easy to slip it into writing and conversation ('quality education', 'quality setting', 'quality standards'), as if everybody would understand exactly what quality means in practice (and agree that this is what they wanted or valued for children). The quality of a car will be judged differently by different drivers according to what they most want (size, style, reliability, economy, top speed). To describe something as a 'quality car' says very little about its strengths or weaknesses. Similarly with a 'quality early years setting', different parents will give different priorities to different aspects of the setting (location, training of staff, programme of activities, approach of the manager, facilities and equipment).

When asked what they think is most important, most parents and practitioners list practical things first – safety, hygiene, quality of the food and sufficient staff. However, they also say that whilst these are essential, they are not enough. What matters most once the practicalities are in place are the staff, what they do and how they interact with the children.

This strong consensus amongst the people in daily contact with the children is supported by research:

> Why do infants, indeed all people, so strongly seek states of interpersonal connectedness, and why does failure to achieve connectedness wreak such damage on their mental and physical health?
>
> (Tronick, 2005: 293)

Penelope Leach emphasises the same central point although she expressed it in terms of how much relationships, another word for 'interpersonal connectedness', matter:

> Children's relationships with the people who take care of them are an important – probably the most important – aspect of the overall quality of child care. Research studies have identified a range of caregiver qualities that make good relationships with young children more likely, including sensitivity, empathy, and attunement. Being cared for by adults whose work is informed by these qualities and attitudes can help babies and young children to feel confident in themselves and encourage them to communicate and talk, think and have ideas, discover and learn.
>
> (Leach, 2009: 193)

To this extent, researchers and writers, practitioners and parents seem to broadly agree about what counts in judging quality. However, when Leach speaks of 'adults', how many adults can this be? How can a team of practitioners work as individuals as well as a team offering each child consistent attention as well as enabling the child to benefit from contact with all the people in a team? And what does Leach mean by 'sensitivity' and 'attunement'?

Consistency partly means that the majority of staff working in a setting 'this month' are still there working together 'next month' and the month after and so on. It refers to staff turnover and the importance of this being low. However, it also refers to a more detailed consistency during each day with regard to how many different people hold and care for each child. If a baby has five nappy changes in a day, for example, and a different person carries out each one, is that sufficiently 'consistent'? If six different people give a toddler her lunch, one washing face and hands, another sitting her in her chair, a third spooning in first course and a fourth pudding with a fifth also taking a turn with the spoon and a sixth wiping her face and hands and getting her down at the end, is that sufficiently consistent?

These questions of who does what with each child in each setting, the number of different people and the details of how they interact, are very practical questions that lie at the heart of big questions about quality. But they raise an even bigger question about what kinds of places early years settings should ideally be.

Most people, watching the interaction between a baby and parent figure, are moved by the intensity of their mutual love affair. Whilst the baby's adoration, delight and playfulness can seem to quickly collapse into sadness or even despair, there is no escaping the intense passion and importance of these interactions. This is how babies are!

But why? Is this intense interaction, like any other love affair, purely for its own sake, unique and irreplaceable, a wonderful part of the human condition? Or does it also have a purpose? Is this interaction, in the form it takes, present for a reason? Does it matter for the child's healthy development? Is there even a place for the word 'love' in discussions about professional practice?

It's called love … actually!

'Care' is the word that is most often used in early childhood settings to describe the role of practitioners who are not 'teachers' in the traditional sense of the word … We are continually reminded that care and education are inseparable … For me, in policy terms, the role of 'carer' has always been cast as a 'cinderella' role to that of teacher/educator. Many practitioners choose a career in nursery nursing because of their desire to form close relationships. A well informed practitioner (with a Masters degree in ECE) recently told me, 'Our babies are so happy and content, they have a lovely time, I love them all so much!' …

Drawing on Noddings' work on the intellectual aspect of caring in relation to ethics of care and education, I want to push the boundaries of 'care' and 'love' further, specifically in relation to babies and children under three. I want to suggest that the work of early childhood professionals involves not only 'care' and 'education' but 'love, care and education'. If this is the case then could it be that for some mothers when they recognise reciprocity at first hand they are able to identify the intellectual experience as an attachment that is fundamentally in tune with their own wants and needs for their child rather than a feeling that is threatening to the mother–child relationship?

(Page, 2008: 181–7)

In relation to early years settings, we can ask these questions in another way. We know that monomarty (infants being cared for by one mother figure) is not a precondition for healthy human development. However, do settings need to be places where *some* features of the parental relationship are provided for each child? These features might include coming to know the child very well, showing the child spontaneity, immediacy and delight in interactions, the ability to be involved in an intense relationship without being overwhelmed by it.

In no way is this to suggest the relationships professional practitioners make with children can be the same as home relationships, but it is to ask whether some aspects of the parental relationship need to be replicated in early years settings.

Are settings for babies and young children best understood as an extension of home, where children meet a wider range of adults and children but are still mainly cared for by a small number of people, in relationships that replicate some aspects of home relationships? Our answer to this question is *yes*. For us, the meaning and implementation of the Key Persons approach is about the organisation and detail of professional relationships to support this model.

As we describe on pp. 9–22, others have argued differently. The uniqueness of home relationships and their importance to healthy development are understood and acknowledged. However, their argument is that there is no need to attempt to reproduce any of the attributes of home relationships when children are away from home. They see early years settings as providing an opportunity for children, from the earliest age, to experience and participate in a network of relationships, with other babies and children as well as adults, that is much broader and more open than within a family. In such a model of the early years setting, the Key Persons approach may well then be seen as unduly restrictive.

The early years setting: a home from home?

Is the job of a practitioner, in a 'good quality' setting, to be rather like a loving parent? Practitioners sometimes speak as if the role is like that of a parent although they are often careful to say it is not the same as a parent. Carol and Mehta, experienced practitioners working in private settings, speak first:

> It's like you are sort of their second mum as such because you're like their parent during the day because you do everything with them that their parent would do with them on a Saturday or a Sunday or any other day that they don't come in so it's like you've sort of really got that back stage role it is sort of similar I suppose … it's a nice feeling of second mum, it's not oh God I'm being his mum again today, it's a nice feeling, it's like sometimes when it's during the week you're sort of on the parents' level in a way, well I suppose that sounds wrong. It's just you see as much of them as their parents do. If they're here from Monday to Friday you see as much of the children as their parents see of them. So I suppose that probably sounds weird but … (Carol, toddler room leader)
>
> (Elfer, 2008)

> You do feel like Mum, especially with baby babies because they're so dependent on you, they're very dependent. They need feeding and they just need attention all the time. They need their nappies done and it's pretty much you do feel like their mum sort of. You don't go to the extreme where we try and take over as their mum but it's just that feeling. I know what it's like to be a mum and it's only after having my son how I can actually put it on the other foot now. Whereas before I never had a baby of my own at home 24 hours a day, it's a little

bit different. But yes you do feel like that sometimes. (Mehta, baby unit manager)

(Elfer, 2008)

These two practitioners seem to be emphasising the similarity of a part of their work to that of being a parent, but *similarity* does not mean the *same*.

In this next extract, Sarah, the leader of a room for 1-year-olds, speaks about the dilemmas of close relationships with children:

> There's that fine line, we are the carers and although the children are very young and they still need that nurturing and that comforting there is that line there so we are protecting ourselves as well at the same time. I mean people like to work with children they're like, I love cuddling, but you have to think about your own actions in a sense as well. If children are upset, yes it's nice to give them a cuddle but a quick cuddle's nice, not a 20 minute cuddle. When I was at college I was taught about not sitting children on your laps and I thought well how could you get it for a child not sitting on your lap? They spoke about the implications involved if you work in a room with people and you've got a child that needs to touch you, needs to feel you and children of that age do, then you need to some-how overcome that in some way, and having a child on your lap for five minutes is ok. You wouldn't sit all afternoon with a child on your lap because that's not ok. If a member of staff in my class was doing that I'd have to be worrying about the bonding they are having with that child because children of that age can become too self reliant on a member of staff and you go to lunch and when you go home they are still there obviously with other staff so they need to be able to gel with all members of staff. So by passing that around equally and not spending too much time with a particular child, all children can be catered for and they can become comfortable with their environment and the members of staff who are looking after them. (Sarah, room leader, older toddlers room)

(Elfer, 2008)

The observations of practice in this room showed how much concern this room leader and her staff felt for the well-being of the 12- to 24-month-olds with whom they were working. However, this extract from an interview with the room leader shows the anxieties she feels about responding to young children's ordinary but vital needs for sustained and consistent human contact with a particular person who knows the child well and who can think about and respond to the child. It seems that she has concluded, partly with the unhelpful guidance from her training, that whilst close relationships are important for young children, they cannot really be provided well in an early years setting. Every practitioner has to be vigilant about physical contact with children. Physical holding and touching should always be motivated by the baby's or child's needs, not those of the practitioner, and be open and accountable, like any other aspect of practice. Physical touch that is disrespectful or abusive is deeply damaging to young children, immediately and in the long term. Child protec-tion policies are an important safeguard. However, it is important to remember too that physical touch is part of human relationships and essential to healthy development in children. Withholding appropriate physical touch and comforting would be as abusive as imposing inappropriate touch.

We know now (not least from some of the examples of very careful, sensitive and well supported practice given in the final chapter of this book) that close *and respectful* relationships *can* be provided well in professional early years settings.

Practitioners generally (and understandably) seem very sensitive to issues of fairness in the way children are treated, fairness in the way work is shared, the importance of working as a team and helping one another out and the dangers of encouraging children's expressions of preference for one member of staff over another. They are usually very aware that being in a professional role that comes close to a parental one will sometimes make parents very anxious and possibly angry, as in this example about Melissa, aged 8 months, her mother, Florence, and Key Person, Lilia:

Lilia had been thinking about one of her key children – something seemed wrong. Melissa had been attending the nursery for about two weeks and at eight months of age had been used to being at home with her mother with whom she shared a very close and loving relationship. Lilia thought about what she knew generally about child development and knew that from about six months of age it is quite usual for babies to show signs of concern when they lose sight of their significant adult and become more wary of strangers. Lilia had tried gently to discuss this with Melissa's mother and to suggest why it might be a good idea for Lilia to gradually form a bond with Melissa. Melissa's mother, Florence, became quite alarmed and said somewhat accusingly to Lilia, 'under no circumstances are you to become close to Melissa, she is my baby do you understand?' Lilia felt nervous and shy and found it difficult to strike a balance between supporting Melissa's need for a close relationship while at nursery and her mother's concern about getting 'too close'. Lilia knew it was vital to be respectful of Florence and her views but she also recognized that not to meet Melissa's needs, if she failed to respond lovingly, could be potentially more concerning in the long term.

This came to a head one evening when Florence arrived early to collect her baby. Melissa was busily engrossed in her play at the treasure basket and Lilia was sitting next to her. Seeing Florence arrive, Lilia got up quickly from the floor to prepare Melissa's bottles and other items which she needed to take home. Melissa protested and started to cry, her mother sat down beside her and lifted Melissa on to her knee but Melissa protested even more, holding her arms out to Lilia who was desperately trying, with some embarrassment, to busy herself preparing the bag. With Melissa still crying in her arms Florence grabbed the bag from Lilia and rushed out of the baby room and bumped straight into Jane, the nursery manager. Noticing her distress Jane said to Melissa 'Oh dear what's all this then?', Florence looked up and said angrily 'I told her this would happen'. Jane invited Melissa and her mother to her office and listened to Florence's concerns about Melissa forming what she described as 'too close' a bond with Lilia … With Florence's permission, Jane asked Lilia to join the discussion … Lilia reassured Florence that she was in no way attempting to replace Florence ... Over the next few weeks Lilia and Florence built a trusting relationship.

(Nutbrown and Page, 2008: 100–1)

Early years practitioners surely meet this kind of fearfulness, expressed in many different forms, many different times. Who would not be very wary of the dangers of allowing, or even unwittingly encouraging, children to blur the boundaries between who is mummy and daddy and who is a special adult in the early years setting? If we were thinking only about Melissa's mother Florence, or her Key Person, Lilia, we might think that the Key Persons approach is really not worth the upset it has caused. But being child-centred means thinking about Melissa's needs as well as those of her family. We think Lilia is absolutely right that not to allow Melissa to make a bond with her could be very harmful.

How important though that Jane had the time and skill to realise Florence's distress needed to be taken seriously, and responded to with time and careful attention. We think this is an example of highly sophisticated and sensitive practice but also an inevitable and essential part of the Key Persons approach.

The early years setting: not a substitute home but a place to be different

Other writers have argued that the early years setting should not, even ideally, be like home.

Gunilla Dahlberg, Peter Moss and Alan Pence radically analyse the place in society of what they call the 'Early Childhood Institution'.

It is impossible to do justice here to the depth of their discussion but from the point of view of relationships *within* the early years setting, the following quotations give the essence of their case against emotional closeness and intimacy:

it is not to be understood as a substitute home. Young children – both under three and over three years of age – are seen as able to manage, and indeed to desire and thrive on relationships with small groups of other children and adults, without risking either their own well being or their relationship with their parents. Not only is there no need to try in some way to provide a substitute home, but the benefit from attending an early childhood institution, comes from it not being a home. It offers something quite different, but quite complementary, so the child gets, so to speak, the best of two environments.

(Dahlberg *et al.*, 1999)

This message is also clear. The 'Early Childhood Institution' is seen as an opportunity for the child to experience quite different relationships with adults and other children than experienced at home. To seek to make the setting like home is to deny the child that opportunity.

The writers go on:

If we approach early childhood institutions as forums in civil society, the concept of closeness and intimacy becomes problematic. It can turn public situations and institutions private. As such, it not only creates a 'false closeness' and risks trying to duplicate, necessarily unsuccessfully … it also hinders the ability of the institution to realise its own social life and relationships.

(Dahlberg *et al.*, 1999)

The argument here is that planning for closeness and intimacy means *over*-managing the relationships of the institution, encouraging some and restricting others. This could perhaps be likened to a social gathering where the guests, rather than mixing freely, remain in pairs or small groups so that the possibilities that might be created from a wider group of people mixing together never really develop. The writers go on to introduce an alternative to individual closeness:

To abandon ideas of intimacy, closeness and cosiness does not leave indifference, callousness or coldness. It does not mean being uncaring. Instead … a contrasting concept to closeness, the concept of *intensity of relationships* implying a complex and dense web or network, connecting people, environments and activities which opens up many opportunities for the young child.

(Dahlberg *et al.*, 1999)

It is this network of relationships and the importance of each child having access to the whole network and not being confined to individual relationships that sharply distinguishes, in their view, the early years setting from the home:

If the early childhood institution is not understood as a substitute home, then the early childhood worker is also not to be understood as in any way a substitute parent.

(Dahlberg *et al.*, 1999)

If this sequence of arguments from an academic perspective is combined with the anxieties expressed by Carol, Mehta and Sarah, all experienced practitioners, there might seem to be a strong case *against* forming special relationships between children and particular early years practitioners.

The arguments against the Key Persons approach could then be summarised like this:

1   It brings staff too close to a parental role and they risk becoming over-involved.
2   If children get too close to any one member of staff, it is painful for them if that member of staff is not available.
3   It can be threatening for parents, who may be jealous of a special relationship between their child and another adult.
4   The Key Persons approach is complex to organise and staff need to work as a team, not as individuals.

5   It undermines the opportunities for children to participate in all the relationships of the early years setting community.

Why should any setting go to the trouble of implementing such an approach in the face of all these apparently good reasons not to?

Relationship is key: the theory

We do not think the above five arguments stand up to scrutiny, or justify the consequences for very young children if they are left feeling that nobody really knows about or understands their feelings. Certainly, the first three arguments are real issues and do involve difficult and painful feelings for adults, parents and professionals. In some of the examples we give in later chapters, practitioners speak quite directly and openly of the painful feelings the Key Persons approach has evoked for them. We think that to speak in this way can be a sign of a highly professional reflection, not of revealing a lack of professionalism.

The fourth reason is also undoubtedly true. It is much easier for heads and managers to be able to change staff between rooms than to have to worry about ensuring consistent staffing for children. But being child-centred means taking account of *which* staff, not only *how many* and just whether the ratios are right.

In relation to the fifth reason, there are indeed powerful opportunities to experience participation in the community of the setting, a microcosm of the wider community in which the setting is located. This experience is very different from that at home and cannot be had at home with the same richness and variety that an early years setting can provide. The opportunity for a child to relate to a much broader group of children and adults than available at home is often stated by parents as a main reason for choosing a group setting. When the Key Persons approach works well in our experience, making friends and participating in groups, even for 1-year-olds, is helped when a child feels secure with his Key Person.

In other words, the Key Person, by being available to children, helps them to feel confident about gradually making friends and participating in groups. The role should not be restricting this important dimension of life in the early years setting. There is a subtle skilful balance to be made between helping a child have the confidence to be adventurous and stretch their capacities (whether taking on the challenge of an activity alone or tentatively forging new relationships with other children) from a secure base with their Key Person, and trying to force the child to do these things by not allowing him to have a secure base with his Key Person in the first place.

Overall, we think the evidence about the nature of human relationships and the longing to form individual attachments, particularly for very young children, is so overwhelming that the arguments to do with feelings and organisation given above become challenges to be overcome rather than reasons *not* to develop the Key Persons approach.

The inbuilt desire of human infants to be in relationship with others is described very clearly by Schaffer (1998):

it is increasingly difficult to avoid the conclusion that in some sense, the infant is already prepared for social intercourse … if an infant arrives in the world with a digestive system to cope with food and a breathing apparatus attuned to the air around him, why should he not also be prepared to deal with that essential attribute of his environment, people?

Alvarez (1992: 73) suggests that intimate interaction is the very way babies come to be aware of the very existence of other human minds and the existence of their own humanity:

I suggest that babies being handled all over, talked to, and gazed at are not only being called into awareness of the human world outside themselves, they are being called into awareness that they themselves exist.

Elinor Goldschmied and Sonia Jackson (1994: 37) describe the deep significance of these special relationships in our everyday lives:

why should it be worth the time and trouble to introduce a Key Person system in a nursery where this has not been the practice? We have to consider the question not only from the point of view of the child, but also from that of the worker who takes on the emotional responsibility. Thinking of our own relationships as adults may give us some answers.

Most of us have, or would like to have, a special relationship with some person on whom we can rely, a relationship which is significant and precious to us. If we are parted from that person we have ways of preserving continuity even through long separations. We use telephones, letters, photographs, recollections, dreams and fantasies to keep alive the comfort which we derive from such human relationships. When we lose them, we experience sadness and often deep feelings of despair. If we look back we may recall important people in our early lives who, though they were not there in person, give continuity and significance to how we conduct our present lives. Often we seek to repeat and enjoy again the warmth of those relationships in a different form.

Here, Goldschmied and Jackson are drawing on attachment theory (Bowlby, 1988) and the importance of attachment relationships for people in every culture (Rogoff, 2003). Felicity de Zulueta, writing as a psychiatrist and a biologist, puts this argument about the importance of particular relationships in a more academic and general context:

What the attachment behaviour in humans keeps on showing us is how important it is for infants and children to become attached to those who care for them: this is both normal and healthy.

By attending to their infant's psychological and biological needs parents, and later nursery staff can provide children with a secure attachment which will enable them to develop fruitful long term relationships and a sense of being valued and lovable. Unfortunately the reverse is also true: by failing to respond in a consistent and sensitive way psychological damage or trauma may be inflicted upon the child's attachment system and the resultant wounding of their sense of self esteem and their capacity to relate and tune in to others.

(de Zulueta, 2001)

Absolutely none of this is to say that babies and very young children cannot thrive in early years settings. The idea that an early years setting inherently poses a risk to early development is now rejected (Rutter, 2002).

In the US, the largest study of the long-term impact of early years day provision is that of the National Institute of Child Health and Development Studies Early Childhood Research Network (NICHD) (Brooks-Gunn *et al.*, 2003: 188). This study shows that the main factors affecting how young children get on later in life are family factors, not factors to do with the early years setting. Children experiencing good quality childcare had better cognitive and linguistic abilities, showed more cooperative behaviours with their mothers and had fewer behavioural problems (2003: 200). By contrast, poor quality childcare was associated with an increase in insecure infant–mother attachment but only when the quality of interactions at home was not good. This adds weight to the early findings of this large study (NICHD, 1997) of a 'dual risk' effect for children receiving poor quality interactions both at home and in their early years settings but also that high quality early years provision provides some compensation when things are not going well at home.

It is important here that the arguments for individual and consistent relationships in the early years setting are not misunderstood, as indicating that home care is 'best'. The evidence is firm that quality of relationships *at home and in early years settings* both matter.

Other writers, from differing academic branches of psychology, build on what is said by de Zulueta and the pivotal role of individual and special relationships. They give us an insight into the detail of why they matter so much. In the following description, the significance of relationships to brain development is highlighted:

Recent research on brain chemistry has found that, starting from birth, the brain is affected by environmental conditions including the kind of nourishment, care, surroundings and stimulations an individual receives. The impact of the environment is dramatic, actually affecting how the brain is wired … During the first three years of life most synapses (connections) are made, and by the age of three, the brains of children are two and a half times more active than the brains of adults The child's brain at three has twice as many synapses than it will eventually need. Synapses that have been activated many times through early experience tend to become permanent, while those not often used tend to be eliminated.

(Schore, 1997)

Environmental conditions matter and there is specific talk here of 'stimulations'. But what kind of 'stimulations' matter? There is no evidence from neuroscience that the 'dense web of relationships' envisaged by Dahlberg *et al.* provides any less stimulation and is therefore any less able to promote synaptic connections that the Key Persons approach to relationships.

However, other studies draw out which particular aspects of stimulation in the infant's environment are important. Colwyn Trevarthen says this:

> It is clear from the beginning that children have a driving motivation to become part of a meaningful world. They want to share interests, … they like being able to share purposes and actions … Children do need affection and support and protection and so on but they need a lot more than that. They need company which is interested and curious and affectionate … I don't want to underestimate what children can discover for themselves. Children are very good at private research. They can do it very well, but they don't do it if they are discouraged, if they feel unwanted or lonely, then they don't explore.
>
> (Trevarthen, 1999)

He argues that the most important features of the environment for the child are the relationships of mutual meaning and understanding that she or he can build, provided the people with whom these relationships are made are 'interested, curious and affectionate'. In principle, why should not such interest, curiosity and affection be shown within the dense web of relationships described by Dahlberg, Moss and Pence?

The answer is that for a baby or very young child, who has not yet acquired the sophisticated tools of verbal communication, the relationship in which interest and curiosity and affection is experienced is a finely tuned one. A baby is delighted and responsive to the minute details of holding and talking done by a mother or other very familiar adult. But even the warm and affectionate holding by an unfamiliar adult, in which there are minute differences of detail (smell, facial gestures, physical handling and tone of voice) can be experienced as completely 'wrong' and delight can be replaced by anxiety, stiffness or distress.

These crucial details of holding are described by Lisa Miller:

> It is quite clear that babies are frightened of falling and that they need the security of feeling nicely pulled together. Inside the womb, they were held from all sides. Now that they are outside, they need moulding and shaping. You can often see a baby who has burrowed into the corner of a cot or crib, as though trying to find a home that will give him shape.
>
> … the baby needs not only physical mopping up but lots of mental mopping up. By this I mean that just as surely as he evacuates his bladder or bowels a baby empties himself of unhappiness. A crying baby is conveying his or her messy misery and needs somebody to receive it. Crying, as I said before, is communication. It has meaning. But a baby's crying needs an adult's emotional and mental equipment to sort out what it means.
>
> (Miller, 1992: 28)

Miller implies that there are two key jobs to be done for babies – of course physical holding, but a kind of 'mental holding' too. We have sometimes seen in early years settings children held *physically* in a way that ensures they will not fall. However, the quality of holding does not convey a sense of the baby or child being thought about or 'held in mind'. Practitioners often distinguish types of physical holding they have seen in their practice, for example babies that are held like 'packages' and babies that are held more closely and sensitively. The importance of being physically held, especially at times of anxiety or distress, must surely be familiar to most human beings. *Who* does this holding cannot be separated from the holding itself. Being held by the 'wrong' person would not have the same effect at all. What makes the right person 'right' is holding in the context of a relationship of trust, reliability, familiarity and respect.

Alongside physical holding, Miller refers to mental holding or mental 'mopping up' and the ability of an adult to receive a baby's communications of distress. Anyone who has worked with babies might at first respond to this by thinking that it is almost impossible not to receive a baby's communication of distress – crying can have a piercing and powerfully disturbing impact!

But Miller is talking about much more than simply 'hearing the sound' of crying, she is talking about the capacity to think about the possibilities of what it might mean (a full and uncomfortable nappy, a hungry feeling, a sore bottom, being overtired or frightened or missing mummy). This search for meaning – the preparedness to try and understand what the baby's crying might mean – seems to be a close part of what Trevarthen describes as a feature of early communication (see p. 14).

Children are enthusiastic to struggle to make meaning of adults' communications and they need to encounter adults who are equally enthusiastic to make meaning of their communication. This is hard work and does not just happen automatically. The energy for meaning making comes from a relationship involving commitment, concern and affection. Can many adults interacting with many babies reliably offer such attuned and sensitive responsiveness?

The evidence from these four different branches of psychology, neuroscience, attachment theory, developmental psychology and psychoanalytic theory represented by Schore, de Zulueta, Trevarthen and Miller respectively, seem to us to build an overwhelming case for children's crucial need for relationship with adults. Could these relationships be the dense web described by Dahlberg, Moss and Pence that avoid 'intimacy, closeness and cosiness'? We believe they could for much older children who have the physical and emotional resilience to seek out the adults they need and who have a concept of time to hold themselves together, in the 'emotional holding' sense Miller describes, until they get home to familiar adults. But we cannot see how the 'dense web' can 'collectively' provide the individual tuning with reliability and immediacy upon which babies and toddlers utterly depend and thrive. And why do we feel this is not possible? Why should these special relationships not be offered by a team rather than by mainly one or two particular designated members of staff? Surely six members of a team offering special care and attention to a child is six times better than this being done by just one or two members of staff? At first sight, this seems a strong argument and practitioners who want to argue against the Key Person principle often use it.

In practice, however, it seems that unless there is specific organisation around the principle of one or two members of staff building special relationships with children, rather than six people building such relationships, *there is an increased risk that these relationships might never occur.* Anybody might change a nappy, greet the child in the morning, help at mealtimes or settle the child to sleep. Such care has been described as 'multiple indiscriminate care' (Bain and Barnett, 1986). This shared team care allows great flexibility of staffing; anybody can do anything, with any child at any time. And although this team care might be carried out with sensitivity and affection, six staff sharing their care equally between perhaps 15 different children tends to result in generalised care that is not closely attuned to any one child. It is also very difficult for any one of these various members of staff to have paid enough focused and consistent attention to a particular child to be in a position to give detailed and focused feedback to parents about their child's day.

A second aspect of the Key Persons principle that is commonly misunderstood is that children will be restricted to relationships with their Key Persons alone and forbidden or discouraged from interacting with other workers. This is to turn the Key Persons principle on its head, with children having to fit in with this method of organisation rather than this method of organisation fitting in with what children need and want. The point of the Key Persons principle is not to restrict children's interactions with other members of staff but to be sufficiently responsive when they want intimacy and closeness with 'their special member of staff or her backup partner'. When they do not want or need that, but prefer to interact with other staff members, then of course it would be wrong to restrict or try and prevent that in any way.

What do children say about the relationships they need?

Relationship is key: children speaking

The story of Sunil is an account of his separation from his mother. Angelina is in a setting where a Key Persons approach has been developed. Graham is in a nursery room where the four room staff are committed to working as a *key group* rather than as individual *Key Persons* (he tells us why this is not 'good enough' for him towards the end of the day). Lastly, Mario, who is 4, is in a nursery in Naples and tells us his feelings about having to leave nursery soon. We do not know how these children might react in the *Early Childhood Institution* of Dahlberg, Moss and Pence. Nevertheless, we think their evidence is compelling.

The following piece of writing is taken from a book by Meera Syal (1997). In this extract she describes her impression of her baby brother *going to* nursery:

Sunil's story

Sunil would be sleeping on her chest, a snuffling milky mass of warm roundness barring the way to her heart. He had to be forcibly peeled off her at nursery every morning and stopped crying only when one of the carers sang Mama's lullaby to him. Mama had written it down in phonetic Hindi and adapted it to the tune of 'Baa Baa black sheep'. If she tried to put him down, he would clamp toes and fingers to any available expanse of flesh or material and if she she left the room, he would cry, not the petulant demanding cry of the child deprived of a toy but great gulping sobs of abandonment and terror which would bring us all rushing to his side … But once in her arms he would become the Sunil the rest of the world saw and loved, a smiling, dimpled, chubby, bitesized morsel of cuteness dispensing infant largesse from his throne, my Mama.

Such a quotation is likely to provoke strongly different reactions in different readers, as illustrated in Figure 1.1.

Why have we included this fictional extract? To bring to life the importance of having a Key Person in the setting. Sunil's story shows the reality and depth of feelings that a very young child may have as part of his or her whole experience of the early childhood setting. But that does not mean that a baby or young child can only be settled and secure with a close family member.

Angelina's story

In this extract of an observation from a study of children in a full-time setting, Angelina, aged 27 months and much older than Sunil, tells us something of her experience *at* the setting:

> they are talking with each other. Joan's gestures and Angelina's responses suggests that they are talking about the leaves blowing off the trees at the end of the garden. Angelina is running at the end of the playground and excitedly watching the leaves spin down from the tree to the ground as the wind blows them off the branches. Joan has at last found an activity which matches Angelina's need for action and engaged her interest. Joan offers her sustained and individual attention at the bottom of the garden. Angelina seems to be having a very enjoyable, animated and exciting time catching the spinning leaves one by one. After catching each leaf, she runs back to Joan to be lifted up with her, and to look again over the wall.
>
> Joan picks up Angelina when she comes to her and holds her lovingly and they watch the other children together. Angelina seems calmer and snuggles into her and watches the children over the other side of the wall sleepily. She seems to be more relaxed than I have ever seen her before.

Angelina seems to be telling us that having Joan close by makes all the difference to her feelings of well-being. Her behaviour, which was often frenetic and destructive, became calmer and playful with Joan's loving attention.

Graham's story

Graham is 16 months and was observed in a private early years setting where he had been attending full time for some six months. In this early years room, there are four staff working with 12 children. The four staff are committed to working as a close team and their Manager supports them in this by ensuring that they are not 'borrowed' to work in other rooms if at all possible. However, the four staff do not want the children to get any more attached to one of them than to the other three.

FIGURE 1.1 Some reactions to Sunil's story.

So they are very careful to discourage preferences and to 'share' their care between the children. In the first observation of Graham, one hour before lunch, he reads with a member of staff. As he fetches new books, there is a good deal of half playful, half mildly aggressive vying for and switching between adults' laps. Graham seems to cope well with this until more firmly excluded from Anne's lap:

> 11.51am: Luke has hurt himself and Anne draws him closer on to her lap. As they read, the very large picture book seems to form a circle with Anne's arm completely enclosing them and with Graham outside this enclosure. But he remains sitting next to Anne, looking now at his own book and just occasionally looking up at her … . Then Anne and Vicky realise that he has poked out the plastic bubble cover protecting the picture book that he has chosen. 'Oh look what Graham has done …'.
>
> A number of interpretations can begin to be constructed from the first observation and kept in mind in thinking about subsequent observations of him. Graham seems to express a need for individual adult attention but also his ability, or the necessity, to manage this in different ways that is alternating between different adults and with different degrees of proximity, sitting on a lap or holding onto Anne's leg. When he cannot actually be on a lap, but only sit adjacent to an adult, physical connection with that adult seems to help reinforce his sense of emotional connection. His confidence to move away from adults when be wants to, for example to get another book, suggests his emotional security with this shared care. However, there are limits to this and when he maybe feels excluded, for example when Anne encircles the hurt Luke, he finds a way of expressing his protest and anger. His feelings of being pushed out are perhaps represented in his own 'pushing out' of the plastic bubbles of the book cover.

Later in the day, Graham cannot manage his feelings in the same way. He begins to seem very tired and also to find it very difficult each time the door opens with a parent or grandparent coming to collect a child but not his parent or grandparent. Once again, the commitment of the staff to team care but also the link between physical contact and emotion shows itself:

> Vicky changes his nappy and he begins to cry. It is only whimpering/moaning crying to begin with but when he is put down, he cries more loudly and persistently. However, Vicky is now getting Christmas cards ready for each parent to take home … As Graham cries bitterly reaching up to her, she steadfastly continues this job … (this expression of preference is not what they want). Graham is not to be deflected so Brigid actually lifts him away and sits on the floor with him. He cries all the louder … Eventually, Vicky completes the Christmas cards and comes to Graham. He lies in her arms and immediately settles.
>
> (Elfer, 2006: 88–9)

Graham seems to communicate clearly that whilst he can manage with any one of this consistent team of four staff in the morning, when he is not too tired or stressed, he feels very different at the end of the day. Then, when he is tired and perhaps anxious as other adults arrive to collect children but he has still to wait, he needs the individual attention of Vicky.

FIGURE 1.2 Some reactions to Graham's story.

Mario's story

Mario was 4 years old.

> On his arrival in the school, the observer found the children gathered in the garden near a wooden house that had been built there. It is a simple house, rather like those in children's drawings, a doorway and two side windows. Mario has a large broom in his hand and is sweeping inside the house and brushing the dust outside. There are three or four children who call his name repeatedly and bring him leaves, asking him whether they are ok. With the broom in his hands, he replies that they will do fine. He wears a light blue shirt and shorts. He looks very awkward with the broom in his hand as it towers over him.
>
> Without stopping sweeping, he comes out of the toy house, comes towards me and tries to hit me twice on the head with the broom.... Mario says that they are in the middle of the sea and that the house is a boat. Then, using the broom, he begins to brush the walls saying, 'Let's wash the windows now'. The children are

very collaborative and the game seems to consist of creating this space – house-boat. Other children gather plants and bring them to Mario … Mario shows 'captain-like' behaviour in this situation …

Mario, who is about to leave the school for good, seems to have become the spokesman for anxieties about separation shared by all children: the captain, the planner and the director of the game. However, it is interesting to note that the children do not use Mario to free themselves of their own anxieties and unload them onto him, as they might have done if they had made him feel excluded and isolated, but associate with him and try to represent their feelings in the group game. With the end of school and the impending separation, there are no longer any fixed points and the important sense of stability offered by the regularity of the rhythms and rituals of school life will cease. The house becomes a boat, the separation, a journey. But these children have clearly found, in their relationship with the teachers and the school as a whole, a positive experience in feeling themselves recognised as individuals and kept together as a group. 'The teachers always manage to find the right thing to say to each one of them' was a frequent comment of the observer. They therefore do not seem to experience the separation in a catastrophic way. They build their Noah's ark, which can bring them to safety, and the first task they undertake is to clean it. 'But what do they have to clean?', we might ask. The experience of separation always reactivates anxieties of being expelled, placed at a distance, abandoned and maybe a trace of these feelings can be found in the sudden and apparently unmotivated gesture on Mario's part when he hits the observer on the head.

These feelings, however, are relatively marginal. The children's central experience seems, in fact, to be that of being able to separate, feeling themselves to be contained and bringing with them supplies made up of memories, emotions and sensations – colours, familiar smells, basil and other plants – experiences which can be transplanted, with the hope that they will root and flower in other places as well, in other contexts, with other people.

(Adamo, 2001: 135–6)

In this observation extract, what Mario may be communicating through his play about his experience at the nursery school is perhaps more open to interpretation than in the examples given before his. The full paper from which the observation extract is taken reports that Adamo observed Mario over a long period so she will have got to know him very well. Her interpretations are interesting. They include the understanding of how much Mario has become attached to his nursery teachers and the anxieties that are evoked in him by knowing that he will soon leave nursery school. However, Adamo also conveys strongly her sense that Mario's experience of close relationships at nursery school have strengthened him and made him feel able to manage the tricky but important task of 'moving on', something that he (indeed all of us) will have to do from time to time throughout life. Although he has to leave the nursery teachers behind, he will take with him, inside, his feeling of their care and attention to him, as a vital resource, as he embarks on 'his continued journey'.

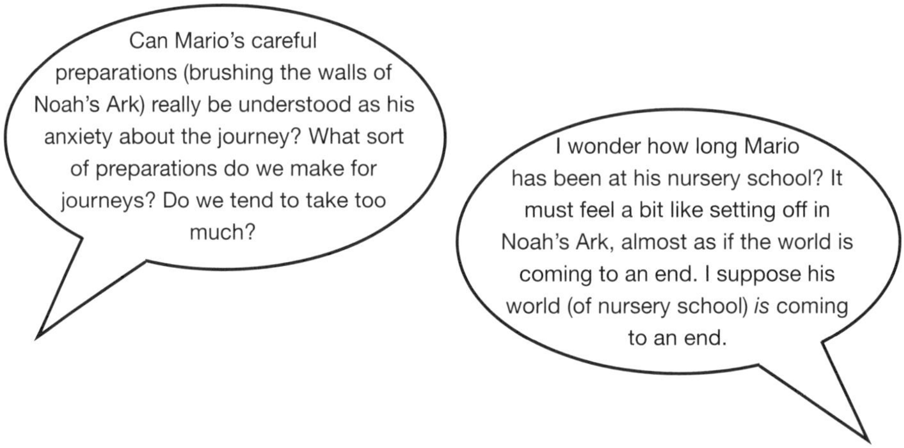

FIGURE 1.3 Some reactions to Mario's story.

How do we respond to these different voices and what they may be seeking to tell us?

Our responses to babies' and young children's powerful communications, for example the baby crying in the supermarket or the toddler rigidly refusing to be strapped into his buggy, are likely to be full of mixed thoughts and feelings. How we react seems to depend as much on our own internal states of stress or calmness, as well as the external circumstances.

But if we put to one side these personal responses, and focus on what children have to communicate to us with their spoken expressions as well as their body language, we think it is almost impossible not to hear two big messages from them to us:

1   How much particular adults matter to them.
2   What a huge difference these adults make to their emotional well-being and their ability to enjoy and learn from the opportunities around them.

What is the Key Persons approach?

The Key Persons approach is a way of working in early years settings in which the whole focus and organisation is aimed at enabling and supporting close attachments between individual children and individual practitioners. The Key Persons approach is an involvement, an individual and reciprocal commitment between a member of staff and a family. It is an approach that has clear benefits for all involved.

The benefits of a Key Persons approach

For babies and young children

The Key Person(s) makes sure that, within the day-to-day demands of the setting, each child feels special and individual, cherished and thought about by someone in particular while they are away from home. It is as though the child was 'camped out in the Key Person's mind' or that there is an elastic thread of attachment that allows for being apart as well as for being together. The child will experience a close relationship that is affectionate and reliable.

For parents

The Key Person(s) approach ensures that parents have the opportunity to build a personal relationship with 'someone' rather than 'all of them' working in the early years setting. The benefits are likely to be peace of mind and the possibility of building a partnership with professional staff where the pleasures and stresses of bringing up children can feel more shared. It gives parents the chance to liaise with someone else who is fully committed and familiar with their baby or child.

For the Key Person

The Key Persons approach is intense, hard work and a big commitment. This relationship makes very real physical, intellectual and emotional demands upon the Key Person and these need to be understood, planned for and supported by each setting's policies and management. One of the benefits of being and becoming a Key Person is that the Key Person will develop a sense of really mattering to a child and to their family. The Key Person is likely to have a powerful impact on the child's well-being, his mental health, and his life chances to think and learn. These powers and responsibilities will engender feelings of pleasure and pain, the joy and relief of partings and reunions, and the satisfaction and anxiety of being a Key Person in a child's formative early years care and education.

For the early years setting

The Key Persons approach leads to staff who are more satisfied and engaged, improved care and learning for the children, and a parent clientele who are likely to develop a more trusting confidence in the competencies, qualities and devotion of professional staff. There are indications that this approach reduces staff sickness and absence, and develops involvement and positive attitudes to professional development within staff teams.

Why 'Key Person' and not 'key worker'?

The terms 'key worker' and 'Key Person' are often used interchangeably in early years work. We would like to draw a clear distinction between the two terms.

The term 'key worker' is often used to describe a role in which the focus is on liaison or coordinating between different professionals or disciplines, making sure that services work in a coordinated way. 'Key worker' may also be used to describe how staff work strategically in the setting to enhance smooth organisation, undertake and coordinate observations, and maintain records and prepare assessments. The 'key worker' role is thus a very important one, essential to effective early years practice.

However, the term 'Key Person' emphasises something beyond this. It refers to a professional relationship that has direct emotional significance from the point of view of the child and his or her family. The essence of the 'Key Person' role is to be someone who is 'key' to the child. Think of the number of personal contacts most of us may have stored in our mobile phones. Despite the large number, it is probably the case that only a very small number of these 'contacts' are people who are really key figures in our daily lives. The 'Key Person' is someone in the early years setting who has real daily meaning and emotional significance to the child and his family.

Early years settings need to hold both these roles in mind, nurturing them, whether they are provided by separate people or are undertaken by the same person.

The Key Persons approach for babies and young children

The first few years, and especially the first 12 months, are a very sensitive, special, exciting, anxious, often overwhelming time for a young child. If nurseries work well, they may be able to provide a deeply satisfying and enriching experience for the youngster. This is not replacing but supplementing the loving care and learning time children need at home.

As babies move towards crawling, toddling and more confident walking, they are also able to seek out the adults they need. The availability of one main adult whom they can count on is very important to them. That person can provide the baby with a sense of being special, even of being loved, secure and thought about.

During our work in a wide range of nurseries, parents often tell us that while they want their child to make special relationships with adults in the early years setting, they would rather these didn't become 'too special'. However close the relationships a child might make in the early years setting, relationships at home are usually the most constant, this being the safest and soundest place from which children may move on to other friendships and connections with many affectionate and interesting people. The key close people in the setting might have to change from time to time, so it is important that parents remain the most stable and strong starting place from which to venture out.

Of course, the Key Person cannot be there every minute of the day; no one, even at home, can manage, or would even aspire to manage, that. Otherwise, how would children ever learn that they could survive if left alone for a short time? How would they realise that the people who love them or who are concerned for them will not forget them but will come back as soon as possible?

Some babies and children are in the setting from around 8 in the morning until 6 in the evening – ten hours. Very few staff work shifts that long and obviously the Key Person will go on holiday, be off sick, or will have to attend to something else during a child's time at the setting. It is at these times that a back-up Key Person is so important. Even so, the periods when the main Key Person is not available must be kept to a minimum or the role starts to have less value.

The Key Person is the staff member who has begun to get to know the important adults and brothers and sisters at home, who knows the baby or young child well and is aware of all the special details of how he or she is cared for and is directly interacting with the child during much of his day. So the Key Person is the staff member who is there, as far as possible, to greet the baby or child in the morning, to provide comfort if he is upset, to play and enjoy time with him, and to be the one, whenever possible, to offer intimate bodily care. This staff member will also have other children for whom she is a Key Person and part of the skill of her job is being available to each of these children, in turn and sometimes together, as much as she can. Of course, the demands of early years setting organisation and the fact that she has only one pair of hands means she cannot do everything for everybody all of the time.

What is certain is that children who are enabled to feel safe and secure will be much more able to be themselves and to try out new ideas in the various relationships and experiences on offer in the early years setting.

The essence of what it means to children to have a 'Key Person' is we think illustrated vividly in the following two vignettes. In the first, Peter Elfer describes his observation of the way in which Tina acts as Key Person to Harry (just past his first birthday), helping him part from his father and settle in his integrated early years setting. In the second, Sarah Hall, a teacher in the foundation class of a primary school, describes the importance of the role for the children in her care.

Harry arrives in his father's arms. He has a round, open, rather solemn face. His Dad is very tall, cheerful and friendly as he enters the room. The family has just arrived back from a holiday in America where Harry has grandparents. Dad passes Harry to Tina who greets him very warmly, holding him slightly apart from her to look at him and welcome him back but also holding him affectionately and firmly – she seems genuinely pleased to see him back. As Dad hangs Harry's coat up, Harry bursts into tears and protests loudly, leaning out from Tina's arms, and stretching towards Dad. Dad laughs, in a gentle way as if to say 'this is not actually as bad as you are making out Harry and anyway, it is just one of those sad things that has to happen in life'. With that he leaves still laughing but also communicating his sense of confidence about the manageability of this separation.

Tina walks with Harry, still crying loudly and very upset, round the room and then says 'I know what Harry likes – doors' and she takes him across to a cupboard and opens the doors but it is clear that Harry is not ready for this distraction. He continues to cry and protest loudly and Tina changes tack and says 'I'm going to take Harry round the garden for a walk' and she leaves the room with Harry in her arms. She seems confident and un-phased by his crying. Within about five minutes, she returns. Harry is still in her arms and he has stopped crying but he still looks sad and close to restarting. But over the next few minutes, he seems to become more contained and Tina takes him over to a little wooden play cooker with pots and pans on top, knobs to turn and doors at the bottom that open like cupboard doors rather than folding down. She sits on the floor with him in front of the oven.

Harry's confidence continues to grow and he begins to play with the oven. He turns the knobs, with fine manipulative control and a three finger tripod grasp of the knob but he is more interested in swinging open the doors of the oven. His energy levels and interest seem to visibly rise in front of my eyes as he gets into playing. His attention switching away from the oven from time to time to watch intently interactions between other children and between children and adults. But the thing that energises him and captures his attention most are the doors. He seems to know exactly how they work, prising his fingers into the little gap between them when they are closed and pulling firmly so that suddenly the right hand door swings open and back on its hinges. His manner is one of determined, energetic confidence about how they work. As the content of the oven is revealed, I strongly expect him to look into the oven at the objects that are revealed there but this is not his interest. Rather, his interest is in the door itself, now in a new position. I wondered if the interest might be in the mechanism of the hinge but it does not seem to be. It is the door, the inner surface now exposed and facing outwards, that seems to intrigue and occupy him. And then the door is swung back again, to the closed position, only for him to experimentally swing it back open again, intrigued by the inner face of the door that has now become the outer face.

Seeming to feel that Harry is more settled, Tina begins to move about more in the room. However, she never leaves him for long, always coming back to be in his proximity. At one point, he crawled away from the oven and used a small chair to pull himself up to a standing position. Then he turned and pushed the chair, pushing it along as a child might push a wheeled brick trolley, perhaps something firm to support him akin to the support he feels from Tina.

He continued to play always with Tina attentive to him or if she was attending to other children, at least nearby. Her attention and proximity seems to sustain him. Occasionally, he would make a loud stream of babbling vocalisations. I could not discern any meaning but language did not seem far off. In contrast to his feelings when he first arrived, he now seems very settled exploring the opening of doors, spinning the knobs of the oven, or the saucepan lid or the wheel of the brio train. It is noticeable that Tina can even move right away from him without him reacting immediately. Only once, when she disappeared altogether from view, having to get something from inside a cupboard, did he purposefully crawl after her, clearly intent on finding her, but without crying.

And then Tina took another child onto her lap, talking to that child and bouncing him up and down whilst singing a nursery rhyme. Harry looked up from his sitting position. His body seems to radiate concentration, interest, pleasure at the rhyme but also an astonished question about why Tina would have another child on her lap. I notice his right leg extend and draw up several times in quick succession but it is not clear at first whether this is a kind of kicking expression of outrage or a different communication of pleasure. But then he does begin to whimper a little and Tina puts the child down and picks up Harry saying 'oh you're getting tired aren't you' and she takes him to change his nappy and settle him into a cot. She soon returns with him still in her arms having decided he is perhaps not quite ready for a sleep but too tired to really be able to continue to play separately from her.

(Elfer, 2008)

It will not always be possible for Tina, or indeed any Key Person, to give such sustained attention to a child. However, in this observation extract, the real meaning of the Key Person role and its immense value to Harry seems inescapable.

In the next vignette, Sarah Hall shows the same immense value of the Key Person role in her description of developing the Key Persons approach with an older group of children:

Our Key Person journey began in October 2008, just over two years ago, when I attended a local authority training course on how to implement the Key Persons approach. Over the past two years I have developed and evolved our approach repeatedly as I have seen the positive impact of the Key Person on the children's social and emotional well-being as well as the development in their learning. Throughout this time the staff team within our class has grown much stronger as a unit leading to many improvements in our practice.

As I begin to write this I immediately feel uncomfortable writing the pronoun 'I' – the Key Persons approach is very much about a team! The activities we do within Key Person groups, our assessment of the children, the times we work within our groups as well as how we continue to change and develop our Key Persons approach, is decided by the staff team and their evaluation of our current practice. Consequently I shall continue to write using 'we' when referring to our staff team (currently includes myself as the class teacher, a full time teaching assistant/Key Person, and a job share teaching assistant/Key Person post for every morning. Over the past two years these members of staff have remained the same; however, we have also worked with other staff members including teaching assistants supporting a child with special educational needs and a volunteer teaching assistant training to be a teacher).

We began by establishing our groups and using these during snack time on a daily basis. We observed the children appearing much more secure and willing to talk within a small group of children they knew well and with a Key Person who was there especially for them. We also noticed how the Key Person knew their own group of children particularly well. As we discussed the children's progress, development and needs we began to tune into our group more than other members of the class. Consequently we felt the use of the Key Persons approach was very beneficial to the children and we developed the use of these group times across the school day. We now use our groups at welcome time at the start of the day, at snack time, circle times, during visits to the school library, and at lunchtimes.

I believe I have always known all the children in my class well and been aware of some of their interests, individual needs, aspects of home life, as well as their likes and dislikes so I didn't think the Key Persons approach would change this or affect my knowledge of the children as individuals. I was wrong. It makes complete sense that you can never really get to know thirty people as well as you can ten! The past two years of teaching using the Key Persons approach have taught me this. I have noticed myself and other Key People working within my class develop more profound relationships with the children. I can honestly state that I have a much deeper understanding of my key children as individuals.

There are many examples of how the Key Persons approach has been beneficial for individual children within our class and how the more in depth knowledge of each child helps us to support their development. For example, one child found it difficult to settle in the mornings and separate from his parents. The Key Person was able to help him overcome this because she knew this individual so well. She knew about his likes, dislikes, family background and his experiences the previous day and was able to talk to him about these to help him feel secure enough to say goodbye to his parents.

One day she would ask him about his swimming lessons the night before or would talk about his little sister and ask him if she had been playing with her dolls that morning, she might talk about his favourite TV programmes, discuss whether he had eaten toast for breakfast the same as yesterday or ask if he was going to play on his bike with his big brother at Granny's house after school today. All these may seem like 'little things' but were important and relevant to that individual child and helped us and him to create a strong link between home and school. He found it reassuring to talk about home and as we observed these conversations taking place it became clearer across the months how this child began to felt more secure and happy to separate from his parents with the support of a Key Person who knew so much about him and was genuinely interested in his life.

Our key group times provide countless opportunities for talking! Since using the Key Persons approach we have found it much easier to identify children with speech difficulties. One particular child was able to talk confidently and clearly with good pronunciation; yet his Key Person noticed that he struggled with pronouncing the sounds 'j' and 'ch' and would look away from the group when saying words beginning with these sounds. This was a minor speech difficulty that may not have been identified without the Key Person, who had spent so much time talking with her group. Once we identified this issue it was discussed with the parent, a referral was made and speech therapy activities were implemented at home and at school. The Key Person was able to ensure these took place regularly and modelled correct pronunciation during many key group activities.

We use feeling fans in our key groups every morning for the children to talk about how they are feeling each day. This enables us to find out things about the children that we might otherwise be unaware of. An example of this is when one of the members of the group told us he was feeling sad because his dog had died last night. The parent of this child had not provided this information and without the opportunity to share this in a small group at the start of the day this may not have been known to the staff. This knowledge enabled the boy's Key Person to focus informal observations on this child throughout the next few days to ensure that he was supported when necessary. She helped him to draw a picture of his dog to keep at home so he wouldn't forget her. The other children in the key group were also particularly kind and friendly to him throughout that day and helped him be involved with play.

Our Key People value the small group times that enable them to get to know the quieter members of the class. These children often lack confidence to 'have a go', share their ideas or speak within the group. The regular group times provide us with the opportunity to notice these children's needs. One of the eldest girls in our class is very shy, has low self-confidence and is unsure about contributing in these group times. Once the Key Person had observed this she decided to complete some observations of the child during child-initiated play. These observations enabled her to discover the child's skills and she noticed how well she was able to draw pictures. The Key Person then used this information during a group conversation about what the children felt they were good at doing and she was able to help the girl to contribute towards the conversation and feel more positive about herself.

We have worked with a child with specific special educational needs whose parents also required some support and reassurance. The Key Person in our class built a strong bond with the parents gradually throughout the school year by talking to them initially about everyday things and then involving them in their child's learning and achievements. By sharing with the parents the activities and strategies we used with their child the parents became more willing to talk to the Key Person and share their own ideas, observations and thoughts. This dialogue became a daily activity that enabled the Key Person to know about the child's home experiences and make links within school. It also provided the parents with ways of talking to their child about school activities. The sharing of techniques and strategies implemented for the child ensured a consistent approach from home and school for the child, which we believe helped him to feel more secure and to understand routines and expectations more clearly. The conversations also encouraged the parents to understand that providing the support for their child was a team approach from home and school and required their expert knowledge of their own child. This Key Person and parent relationship and the positive impacts it had on the child's learning would not have taken place without the Key Person's interest in the child and concern to help him feel secure and happy at school. The extent of the impact of this relationship was demonstrated by a Christmas card and present from the parents given to the Key Person in the term after the child had completed a year at school and had moved to Year One. The parent was very clear that she felt her child's progress was a direct result of their relationship with their Key Person.

We have noticed at the start of the school year each new cohort of children will talk about feeling worried or unsure about lunchtimes. At lunchtime the children eat in the school hall with Key Stage One children and are supervised by lunchtime supervisors. During the two school years operating a Key Persons approach, each Key Person identified children who were concerned about this time in the school day. This year we have extended the use of our Key Persons approach to address this issue. Each Key Person now takes her group of children into the hall and seats them together as a group ten minutes before lunchtime starts. She spends ten minutes settling the children, talking about what food they have, and ensuring the children are happy. A lunchtime supervisor specific to our class then takes over the role of supervision for the lunch hour. This strategy has worked well. The Key Persons are no longer concerned about their group during their break, the children are happy because they know the lunchtime supervisor is there specifically for them and the children are more confident seated within a group of peers that they know particularly well. It also provides a different opportunity for the Key Person to learn about the children in their group. Knowing that a child only likes jam or cheese in their sandwiches gives you a starting point when discussing favourite foods and can also be helpful when trying to settle a child at lunchtime!

The establishment of Key Person groups has been helpful in providing children with opportunities to make friends and develop working relationships with their peers. The children enjoy spending time within the same, small regular group. This September many of the children starting school did not know any other members in the class. Key groups gave these children the opportunity to get to know a few children well to begin with. Observing these children at the start of term showed that they tended to choose to be with children in their group during child-initiated play until they became more familiar with the classroom and other peers in the class.

It is through the Key Persons approach that learning within our class has become more individualised. It is the Key Person who knows exactly which numbers or letters a child is learning to recognise, which child in their group is learning to say 'I' correctly in a sentence, who is developing their ability to sit still and look at the person who is talking and which child always confuses a triangle and a square. The Key Person will often address these aspects of learning on a daily basis for the children in their group. This can take place at any time during the day, including outside, in an adult led activity, during child-initiated play, walking to the hall, during circle time or during key group time.

We believe it is the individualised learning needs like these which, when addressed frequently and regularly in a variety of ways, in various settings and situations and by a Key Person who is interested in the child, help children to make good progress. This has also been shown by the increase in our Early Years Foundation Stage Profile scores since implementing our Key Persons approach. Our scores last year showed an increase in achievement in many areas, particularly within personal, social and emotional development.

What about the Key Person? We believe the Key Persons approach is clearly extremely valuable to the children in the class but it is also advantageous to the Key People themselves. The Key Persons approach has enabled us to view everybody's knowledge of the children as equal and everyone's suggestions and ideas as valuable. We are now a stronger staff team who value each other and enjoy learning from one another. The Key People in our class comment that being a Key Person 'makes you feel better about yourself', 'gives me the self-confidence that I can do it!', 'makes us more attuned to the children and their needs', 'makes us more approachable for the parents' and 'I feel I have achieved something and made a difference to the child and their parent.'

The moment that totally convinced me that the Key Persons approach was not only the 'right thing' to be doing but is actually the most important part of teaching in the early years, struck me last July at the end of the summer term. After completing a school year of using the Key Persons approach as a major part of our daily routines it was clear to all staff, children and parents involved how strong the bonds between all these parties had become. Many parents were obviously proud of their child's achievements throughout their first year at school but it was noticeable how many parents commented on their child's personal, social and emotional development. They were pleased by achievements such as learning to speak aloud to a group of children, being able to pronounce the letter 's', knowing the names of all the children in their group, having the confidence to ask an adult for help, being able to operate independently within the classroom, initiating their own ideas for play, understanding when they were feeling sad and being able to express their feelings, and so the list goes on. The parental thank-yous at the end of the year were directed to their child's Key Person. Many parents expressed their beliefs that their child would not have achieved these things without the support and work of their Key Person who knew their child so well.

Parental support for the Key Persons approach was also demonstrated by the parent who volunteered to talk at the parents' meeting for the new cohort of children. She commented on how supportive the Key People were and how well they knew the children. She explained how before her son started school she was worried he would not be able to carry his school dinner, be able to put his shoes on or know who to ask for help. She said that the Key Person knows their children really well, and helps and supports them to achieve these small but important steps in their learning.

I am convinced that the Key Persons approach is very important for the children in early years. I wholeheartedly believe that both adults and children cannot reach their full potential unless they feel safe, secure, valued and happy. The Key Persons approach has enabled us to heighten the need for this and work towards improving this in our classroom. Key People know their key children well enough to support them to feel this way. I also believe that individualised learning is extremely valuable in helping young children to achieve well at school. The Key Persons approach provides us with an in-depth knowledge of our key children and allows us the opportunities to address individual learning targets. How can we create individualised learning environments if we do not know the children as individuals?

Finally I believe the implementation of the Key Persons approach has encouraged a strong team approach to learning in the early years where the children, Key Person, teacher and parents are all members of the team with an important role. The Key Persons approach is a journey, probably without an end! We have developed, extended and changed our approach over the past two years and will continue to do so as we work with different adults and children and encounter various challenges and (hopefully) have new ideas too! Throughout our journey so far we have learnt it is the Key Person who notices and remembers the smallest details that makes the biggest difference to the individual child's learning journey. It's the little things that matter to young children and they need a special person to care about those little things!

(Sarah Hall, foundation stage teacher, Stockham Primary School)

FIGURE 2.1 Key group time in a quiet space in the school library.

FIGURE 2.2 The Key Person with her group at lunch time at the start of the year.

FIGURE 2.3 Talking about feelings in a Key Person group.

FIGURE 2.4 Time to talk to key children individually.

The Key Persons approach for parents

> It was wonderful to leave him with someone we trusted completely. We knew she understood the real William. She gave him the time and the right encouragement to develop his confidence and become the chatterbox that he is at home.
>
> (Glover and Glover, 2001)

Similarly, Leach and her colleagues, in a paper exploring the complexities of parents' decisions and feelings about choosing an early years' setting, show how important the Key Persons approach would be for some mothers who wanted a group setting:

> Being in someone else's home, you just don't know what goes on all day. I wanted her in a nursery where I could be sure she would be with lots of other children and get lots of stimulation.

By contrast, other parents avoided nursery because they feared their child would not receive individual attention:

> I wanted Alicia to have someone she could directly relate to – form a close relationship with – rather than being in a nursery with lots of different people looking after her.
>
> (Leach *et al.*, 2006: 471–502)

The decision to relinquish part of the care and teaching of your baby or child to the staff in an early years setting is a big step. This leaves some parents feeling anxious and uncertain. Ideally parents would be in a position to help their baby or child settle into the setting with great sensitivity and empathy, but if parents have not had sufficient opportunity to get to know and trust the staff, then their anxiety and uncertainty about leaving their child in a setting with which they are not sufficiently confident may make it doubly difficult to help their child manage the separation in the best possible way. Babies and young children, fearful or anxious about whether this new situation will be safe enough for them, will certainly pick up on their parents' similarly fearful or anxious feelings.

The parents may find it hard to leave or, when they have left, feel very distracted and worried. Sometimes the anxiety and uncertainty seem to have the opposite effect and parents might appear almost too casual to staff, perhaps even a bit uncaring, as they want to flee the pain of being upset or seeing their child's distress by hurrying through any settling-in time. At other times, parents may feel nothing but delight and relief when their child joins in with the activities of the setting almost without a backward glance. However, this very same scenario may just as easily evoke feelings of abandonment, jealousy and secret resentment at the ease with which their child is embraced by the Key Person and other staff and leaves their home attachments.

These different ways of feeling and behaving are means of coping with the act of parting and with any feelings of guilt, anxiety and resentment that may go with it. The Key Persons approach should help manage these feelings. The Key Person can help to make the parting a dignified and carefully thought-out time, even if it is quite a brief affair, rather than a hurried, embarrassed handing-over and rushing away. This will enable the mother or father to feel reasonably confident that they have made the right decision in placing their baby or child in a particular setting. It will reassure them that their child will be well looked after by mainly one person who will help them to keep in touch with their child.

Beyond this important time of settling in, it is vital that parents have an opportunity to build a close relationship with their child's Key Person as this provides a means through which their concerns may be taken into account by the setting. Elinor Goldschmied and Dorothy Selleck have represented these close relationships in the form of a triangle shown literally, but emotionally, containing some of the feelings that arise between families and early settings, as work with children is shared:

Some parents, while valuing what the setting gives to their child, also speak of a slight sense of missing out on what their child does each day. Part of the Key Person relationship for parents is knowing that 'someone', rather than 'all of them', is particularly looking forward to seeing them and talking with them as they hand over or reunite with their child. It is knowing that there is a personal service that will enable their child to go gently from 'one lap' at home to another in the early years setting.

This is where parents' personal stories of their bad night or the thrill of seeing their child's first experiences (of a waterfall, a new rhyme learnt, or their preoccupation with emptying the wastepaper bin) may be shared with humour, with empathy, or in seriousness, and in shared affection for the child. In response, the child's Key Person uses this time to pass to the parent a snapshot of their child's day. Not only the

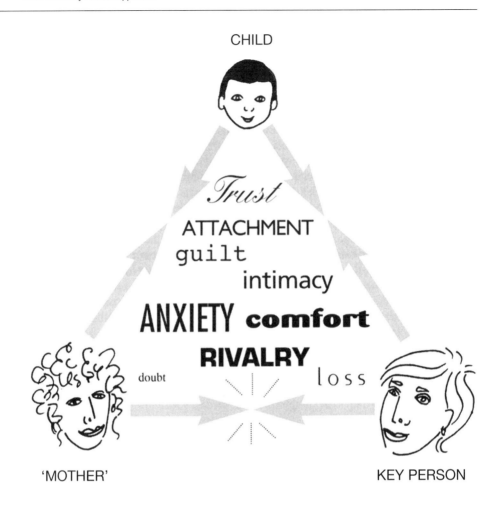

FIGURE 2.5 The 'mother', child and Key Person create and maintain a triangle of trust and communication between each other.
Source: Goldschmied and Selleck (1996).

efficient information of meals eaten and things played with (an important part of customer client services), but more importantly, a personal story from someone they trust to tell them the things they really want to know about. Parents in a Key Person relationship will be able to be in a conversation with that special person. This kind of conversation with a parent can even be worth staying late for as the Key Person will hear some of the details rather than the 'developmental report'. It can be infinitely more satisfying than the parent urgently communicating the essentials to 'the staff' as their employer/customer in the early years setting service.

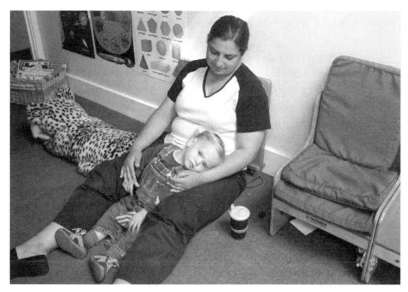

FIGURE 2.6 A child being settled into the early years setting. After separating from his parents, the Key Person stays physically close and available to the child. The child has time to take in the surroundings and time to choose where to play next, as he is held safely in the comforting, containing lap of his Key Person. His special toy and drinking cup are close by to sustain connections with home, and the Key Person observes and holds him attentively as he looks inquiringly, warily, at the other activities and people in the early years setting.

FIGURE 2.7 A child and her Key Person enjoying play together in the outside learning area. This is a special person to share her excitement with as she makes new discoveries and learns new skills. Later she may go on to play with other children and other adults as she gains confidence in her play with the new tyre game.

The Key Persons approach for the Key Person

> In a recent questionnaire, staff were asked about their feelings about working in the centre. Almost all staff expressed a high level of satisfaction in their work, and commitment to children and families in their Key Person groups, and to their own continuing professional development. The ability to plan and care for their own group of children motivated staff who frequently described themselves as 'happy' in their work.
>
> (Duffy, 2000)

For members of staff, the Key Persons approach can make their job much more satisfying. There is evidence of fewer absences, and staff are less likely to move on when they experience the particular responsibilities and pleasures of being involved with a few children in particular. We also know that this special relationship between child and Key Person in the setting does not compromise the close bonds between parents and children at home (NICHD, 1997). The parents will always be the most significant people in a child's life and personal interactions between staff and parents – where trust, as well as anxieties (mistrust), can be spoken about – can be professionally challenging and worthwhile.

Looking after someone else's baby on a day-to-day basis in an early years setting is a complex job involving a great deal of 'emotional labour', responsibility and trust on all sides (we say more about this on p. 61 of the next chapter). We believe that it only really works well for the staff when this is recognised, talked about, and supported. There is all too often little recognition of the sustained physical, emotional and intellectual demands made on the Key Person. The physical demands of the day are also considerable and can be reduced by reviewing how lifting and carrying is undertaken and whether it is being done unnecessarily. The emotional demands are great too.

The Key Person is in a professional role but she must develop a very personal and intimate relationship with each of the babies and children with whom she is working. There are bound to be some painful feelings involved, as the work cannot be done really well in an emotionally anaesthetised way. Building individual relationships with children before helping them to move on when it is time to leave, and always being mindful that the parents are the most important adults in their lives, are just two aspects of the job that are bound to touch some of a Key Person's own personal experiences of close relationships, beginnings and endings. Sometimes staff speak of 'loving a child to bits', then in the next breath talk of all the children in only a general and vague way. Maintaining an appropriate professional intimacy, which every child needs in order to feel special, while keeping an appropriate professional distance, requires professional practice, intellectual and emotional, of the highest calibre.

The Key Persons approach for the early years setting or school

The Key Persons approach provides a focus for the organisation of the early years setting. Experience of existing systems suggests that staff are more satisfied and engaged. When staff have an attachment to particular children – rather than merely an affectionate interest in all the children in their room group – they are less likely to need time off from the stresses of managing many children at once. Fewer staff absences and lower staff turnover mean benefits all round for settings; there is more opportunity for continuity in developing good-quality policies and practices, and greater retention of more experienced staff (Raikes, 1996; Hay, 1996).

Professional intimacy and stability in the relationships between adults assigned to small groups of particular children are also likely to provide better care and learning experiences matched to children's cultural and developmental needs (Munn and Schaffer, 1993; Hopkins, 1988; Geddes, 2006; Nutbrown and Page, 2008).

Parents are likely to develop greater confidence in the competencies, qualities and commitment of the setting as a service. When families are involved with a particular worker, who is systematically supported and managed by more-experienced and well-trained professional managers, the professional status and standing of a setting in the community is likely to be enhanced (Raikes, 1996).

A strategy for implementation
An approach, not a system

In this chapter we describe four aspects of establishing the Key Persons approach (illustrated in Figure 3.1) which, during our work with early years setting heads, leaders and managers, have emerged as at the heart of achieving a growing and evolving Key Persons approach that has meaning and significance for those involved in it.

Building anything, including effective practice in early years work, depends on good foundations. The starting point of the Key Persons approach needs to be based on a firm grasp of the values, principles and research evidence presented in Chapter 2. Practical experience has shown that such a way of working, while paying dividends, does not make for an easy life in terms of the organisational and emotional demands that are raised.

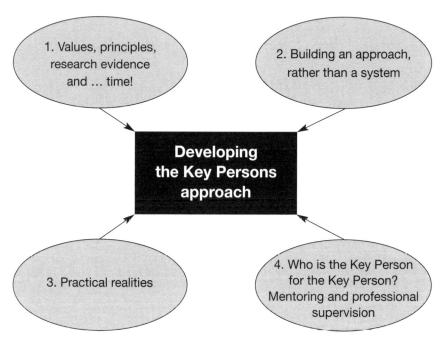

FIGURE 3.1 Implementing the Key Persons approach.

Aspect 1: Values, principles, research evidence and … time!

Each setting should set aside time to read and think about the research evidence presented in Chapter 2. Reading about the importance of relationships in early childhood is an essential part of professional development. Elinor Goldschmied always reminded us about the importance, alongside journal papers and textbooks, of what she referred to as 'internal textbooks'. By this she meant drawing on our own experience, not necessarily at its face value, but our experience tested by our careful reflection, the reactions of those closest to us who may know something about our own early experience and the impact it had, but always valuing it as a source of knowledge and understanding. From here, Elinor argued that we could be stronger in thinking, with the help of external as well as internal evidence, about the significance of building special relationships with the children for whom we have a professional responsibility.

We know from our experience that in most early years settings, from small private nurseries to large integrated nurseries and Children's Centres, time is extremely limited. Very few settings have regular or scheduled meeting time, and maintaining the required ratios is a continual challenge. Staying behind at the end of a shift for a team meeting is exhausting. Building in professional development time for all practitioners, as part of the working week rather than in addition to it, must be a priority, as well as one of the standards by which we compare our national system of provision with that of other countries. Sadly, we are not at that point yet in the development of early years policy in the UK. Nevertheless, individual practitioners and individual settings do seem to manage to be extremely creative in finding ways, often at personal cost, to make space for thinking and discussion. We know this is not always possible but do hope you may feel able to find a way of creating some thinking and discussion time with your colleagues.

From time to time, heads can manage to release a member of staff to join a working group with representatives from other settings; alternatively, it is done at the end of shifts in staff's own time. Sometimes, in larger integrated settings, there may be periods of time during the day or week when there are fewer children in the setting, at which point a small group of staff can meet together.

There are also examples where this process of linking research and practice has been facilitated by bringing in specialist consultants to lead professional development sessions for practitioners to update their knowledge and understanding of the Key Persons approach. Solid and up-to-date knowledge of the rationale of the approach – and dissenting views – will inform and support the planning of heads and leaders before they begin working with their staff teams.

The 'statement of commitment' shown in Figure 3.2 comes from a London nursery's handbook. Research evidence is crucial, but research papers are not normally accessible and easily absorbed so that staff can turn them into practice the next day! The research evidence needs to be digested and turned into a 'working statement' that can be understood by parents and staff as a statement of 'our approach':

What is a Key Person?

What is a Key Person? The Key Person is the special member of staff who comes to visit you and your child at home (if you would like a home visit), who gets to know you and your child, and who welcomes you and your child to the nursery. The Key Person will never ever replace the parent, but will be a special extra adult for your child. We believe that this essential attachment should be planned for and encouraged. As your child gains confidence, then she or he will move happily away from the Key Person and start to get to know the other staff in the nursery. But the Key Person is still there, for you and your child, as a special person who gets to know you and who is there whenever she or he is needed.

FIGURE 3.2 Statement of commitment.

Source: Woodlands Park Nursery Centre's Information for Parents.

Aspect 2: Building an approach, rather than a system

We have referred to the Key Person as an 'approach' rather than a system in order to emphasise that it is about relationships – relationships between children, early years practitioners and family members. Practitioners' relationships with children and families are professional ones with all that 'professional' means – training, working within accepted procedures and practices, continuing and shared critical reflection on practice, openness and accountability. But these relationships in the early years are personal too. It is each practitioner's individuality, personality, warmth and empathy, combined with professionalism, that is the most precious resource for children and families.

There is beginning to be more writing in the early years literature about the importance of this combination of 'professionalism' and 'personal individuality'. It is based on recognition that professional work with the youngest children is not 'professional' in the sense of having a detached, clinical distance. Rather, 'professional' in an early years context means a combination of all the traditional and well-accepted professional attributes *and* recognition of the role of deeply personal interactions and feelings.

Julia Manning-Morton, in an article called 'The Personal is Professional', puts it like this:

> in order to sufficiently meet the needs of very young children and thereby develop quality provision, early years practitioners must develop a professional approach that combines personal awareness with theoretical knowledge … the development of such abilities is enabled in process-orientated training over an extended period of time.
>
> (Manning-Morton, 2006: 42)

Maria Robinson writes about some of the difficult feelings evoked by early years work:

> In order for professionals to work effectively with babies, young children and their parents, their first duty is to recognize themselves for who they are, what they believe and why. The emotions we see in infants and young children do not only belong to them, they belong to us. We have all been helpless infants, we all carry with us our history including that of being parented and therefore, consciously or unconsciously, we know what children are going through at any particular time. When we watch a small child enter the nursery school gates for the first time, we may suddenly be transported back to our own first days at school.
>
> (Robinson, 2003: 171)

Whilst Jools Page speaks of the role of 'love' in early years professional practice:

> I propose that if the government is really serious about supporting the very youngest children and if every child really does matter that 'professional love' needs to be explored and discussed openly and honestly within the early years qualification framework and in the context of other early years policies, alongside and with as much importance as 'leadership and management', cognitive development' and 'phonics'. Let's start talking about loving babies and young children.
>
> (Page, 2008:187)

In other words, not the kind of love where theory, evidence, accountability and critical reflection is lost, but love (and perhaps sometimes 'hate' too) where intense feelings in early years practice can be acknowledged and thought about.

We think this growing attention to the 'personal' and the 'professional' in early years practice is very important in developing the role and practice of the Key Person and an essential part of how the 'Key Person approach' is understood. We say more about this in the final part of this chapter.

Getting the right kind of Key Persons approach underway needs some definite action by heads, managers and practitioners, motivated and driven by a spirit of advocacy to meet the well-being of children. Our experience is that because of the emotional demands of the Key Person role, there will always be a tendency to shy away from it. In the following quotations, two practitioners describe their experiences of attachments forming:

> Tracey: 'On Tuesday this week, Amanda was on her way to work in the Baby Unit, when she was knocked off her scooter. She wasn't badly hurt, although the scooter was a write off, but she'll be off for a couple of days. Jacob is only just one and he's so linked himself to Amanda. He just wouldn't settle when he arrived this morning and although I tried to cuddle him, he just went all stiff – I know he just wanted Amanda – not me. It was horrible for him and it's a horrible feeling too when they don't want you. You have got to work hard in nursery to get the

children to be used to all the staff and to be able to manage with all the members of the team. You can see the problem if they get too attached to one person'.

Leanne: 'It's a bit the same with Amos. As you know I am not permanently in any of the three baby rooms because as manager I am more floating. But Amos, who is nearly two, is so insistent that I somehow belong to him and that he can be on my lap whenever I go into the room. I've always got a group of three or four of them round me but he just pushes his way on and I have to put him off because my lap is just not big enough for them all and it's not fair to let just one … But he makes such a fuss – he's lovely but it really is quite a lot of trouble to handle that every time I go into that room. Tracey is right, we do need to work as a team and they do need to be able to manage with each member of the team, otherwise it's not really fair to them.'

(Elfer, 2008)

If you are reading this not having worked with the Key Persons approach or in an early years setting with such young children, you may think these practitioners are perhaps not very well trained, or experienced or theoretically grounded. If you have worked with the Key Persons approach, you may have experienced similar feelings and feel that their reservations are well justified and that there is a strong case to be made against the Key Persons approach.

The demands on practitioners when children get attached have been well known for over 20 years:

Many of the nursery nurses had experiences early in their career of developing an intense attachment to a child and they still vividly recalled the pain caused to them and to the child when they parted. They also had had experiences of children becoming attached to them demanding excessive attention and being jealous and possessive; they wondered if they had spoiled them. And although they were uncertain whether an intimate relationship with a nursery nurse weakened a child's relationship to his mother, they were very much aware that some mothers became jealous of their children's affectionate relationship to their nursery nurses. So although the nursery nurses expressed themselves in favour of closer relation-ships, they also feared the consequences.

(Hopkins, 1988: 102–3)

Despite this knowledge and despite the known value to children of close professional relationships with practitioners, we still do not seem to be very good at helping prac-titioners manage the painful feelings that attachments with children may evoke from time to time. It is perhaps not surprising then that many early years leaders and prac-titioners either avoid implementing a Key Persons approach in which close relationships are really fostered. We still often hear statements like 'Oh, we all work with all the children and we all get on equally well', or hear reasons to justify saying that it is not possible to have a Key Persons approach at all.

Aspect 3: Practical realities

So what are some of the nuts and bolts of putting the key approach, as we have described it above, into action? All the early years heads and managers we have spoken to said that there was not a blueprint. The process of implementation depended not on any 'right decision' but rather on a continual determination to keep the Key Persons approach on the agenda. In practice, this involved continually moving back and forth between principles, evidence and statements of commitment on the one hand, and solving practical questions, within each nursery's particular circumstances, on the other.

The head or manager will not have all the answers – she faces some difficult challenges. Part of the Key Persons approach is the process of working and struggling together to:

- hear everyone's point of view;
- help each other develop ideas and possibilities;
- put proposals into practice and try them out;
- build on what seems to work and find another way when something does not.

But this must be maintained as a shared responsibility. Practitioners rightly expect to be consulted about and involved in decisions regarding professional practices. One manager told us that, having done this, some staff responded by saying, 'Well you're the manager – you decide.' But being the one 'to decide' is not realistic. The approach does need a 'shared commitment'. Here are some of the key elements of such a commitment.

Introducing the Key Persons approach in different kinds of setting

In the following three examples, we focus on particular aspects of developing the Key Persons approach, in different kinds of early years setting. The first example is taken from a group of private nurseries while the second and third examples are from individual settings. These are three examples of settings in very different circumstances and at different stages in the development and sophistication of their approach.

Example 1: A nursery group

A group of private nurseries with branches across England decided to establish a Key Persons approach in each nursery.

The nursery group created the key national post of Director of Quality and Training to strengthen standards and to provide customers with the best possible service. Most customers are working parents requiring full-time day care for babies through to 5-year-olds.

The company appointed an experienced nursery manager with a recent Master's degree in Early Childhood Studies. Her brief was to develop a high-quality service through a coordinated, professional development training programme. She identified her priorities by:

■ carrying out an audit of the training needs of *all* staff, as identified by them and their managers;

■ identifying the theoretical underpinnings for the design of the Quality Programme, based on her recent study and review of the latest research, as well as taking account of the company's existing ethos;

■ sending all parents a questionnaire: what were their expectations of quality in the nursery?

The Director of Quality and Training was able to identify key responses from which the company's Key Persons approach was developed. Her findings revealed that parents:

■ wanted continuity of care for their babies with as few changes in personnel as possible;

■ valued the connection with 'one of them' rather than 'everyone' when handing over their little children;

■ wanted a person they could contact by phone and text message, as well as the person-to-person contacts at the beginning and end of the day;

■ needed a reliable, dependable and flexible service so they were 'free' to concentrate on work;

■ wanted to know there was someone there who 'loved their babies too, and who *really* listened to what they wanted for their children'.

These responses – which reflected the Director's personal and professional convictions – provided the motivation and commitment to implement a Key Persons approach. They were seen as being at the heart of developing a high-quality and distinctive nursery practice. Her personal charisma and professional authority have been central to the company developing a Key Persons approach.

Next, she designed a staged programme for the implementation of this new approach:

1   A series of meetings with the sales and marketing team was arranged to develop a strategic approach to promote a quality service attuned for children and parents through the Key Persons approach. Establishing the Key Persons approach as a *selling point* should *underpin* the quality of the service. They agreed to redesign their printed marketing material to incorporate an explanation of the Key Persons approach, citing the benefits for parents and children, as well as the commitments needed for parents to plan for an extended settling-in period. This was judged important if the nursery was to remain competitive. It was also agreed that staff handling initial enquiries from prospective customers would have some basic training in explaining this new approach.

2   A series of training programmes for nursery managers was designed to induct them to the theoretical underpinning of a Key Persons approach; to discuss the implications for the deployment of personnel and resources; admissions of children; and the design of a staff training programme.

3   The company decided to introduce the new approach gradually, after staff had been trained and were ideologically and technically prepared for this new way of working. The management team worked hard to consider the implications of these changes. They endeavoured to predict issues to be addressed at each stage without wavering from their resolution to overcome the practical difficulties in the best interests of the children. For example, they anticipated pressures from within settings, to accelerate the settling-in time. The sales and marketing staff – as well as the practitioners – anticipated pressures from parents to 'hurry through' a settling-in process. Understandably, everyone wanted to make the nursery seem as easy and flexible to use as possible for potential parent customers. Establishing how available and flexible parents can be during their child's settling-in period might seem like being a 'nuisance' and an unnecessary complication for a parent trying to meet work commitments. This needed to be addressed in training at all levels.

We want to emphasise the care and attention to detail the company took in laying the groundwork for making the Key Persons approach effective. They achieved this, in particular, by:

■   seeking the views of parents on their expectations of the nursery;

■   enabling the development of a clear theoretical underpinning to the Key Persons approach;

■   explaining the benefits of the approach for parents and children, and being realistic about its demands;

■   anticipating the pressure to 'hurry through' the settling-in period.

In the second nursery, the development of the Key Persons approach is more advanced.

Example 2: A new early years centre

The Key Persons approach in this centre began with reorganisation: staff from a social services nursery joined with staff from a nursery school with the aim of forming a new early years' centre.

The new staff team had a number of team-building sessions as part of a planned process to unite the two different cultures of 'care' and 'education'. Managers decided that all staff would work in cycles with the whole age range of children (18 months to 5 years old). This was met with cautious optimism by some and resistance by others! However, a policy was developed based on the belief that continuity of curriculum as well as constancy in personnel was the bedrock for meeting the needs of children. Many children and families had experienced difficult transitions and family crises. The centre accommodates a wide range of family needs including those of asylum seekers, refugees and families in turmoil with health or social pressures, as well as those of families where both parents chose or needed to work. The staff identified a Key Persons approach as important for children and families, as well as a way of enhancing a 'joined-up' working ethos and practice for the two staff groups becoming one.

In this centre, children are allocated a Key Person who settles them when they begin at 18 months, and then continues with them as they progress through the centre. The Key Person will then stay with the children and support them with their transition into a primary school. This innovative work offers an example of the organisational challenge as well as commitment to the theory and practice of this way of working.

The principles of the Key Persons approach are maintained and the challenges met by a Development Team made up of the senior management team, representatives from the staff working directly with children, and an outside mentor/consultant. The team worked together on practical issues from admissions through to curriculum, and met regularly to review progress.

The discussion notes from one of these sessions, recorded in Figure 3.3, illustrate the range and detail of issues covered in these Development Team meetings and may offer foci for practical developments in other nurseries.

In this second example, there are many detailed 'organisational challenges' for the senior management team. These present an important contrast to the careful ground-work being carried out in the first example. We think the care taken to address these challenges is crucial to how well the Key Persons approach is working out in practice. This example shows clearly how each setting needs to solve its own organisational and practical issues of implementing and monitoring its Key Persons approach if all staff are to be involved in, and committed to, 'making it work'. These two settings show different approaches and different stages of the development process. We also see how the professional teams are identifying and documenting the tasks they need to do next.

Example 3: A small private nursery

As with the centre in Example 2, it was an external event that created the opportunity, or rather the *need*, to develop the Key Persons approach. Example 3 is a privately owned nursery, and offers full- and part-time places to 42 children aged between 4 months and 5 years. The owner/manager established the nursery in her own home, offering places to 21 children. As a home-based nursery, it reflected the owner's personal ethos: small, intimate and homely, with each child and family well known to each member of staff. It also allowed these close relationships between staff and children to develop without the need for active organisation and systems to make this happen.

But an expanding nursery based in the home of a growing family is bound to lead to pressures on emotional as well as physical space. In February 2001, the nursery moved to premises that offered a separate physical space, as well as enough extra space to double the numbers of children. The owner/manager was presented with a tremendous sense of opportunity but also faced the risk that the closeness and intimacy of nursery relationships built up in a home environment, and developed over nearly a decade, would be lost.

The individual relationships that had arisen so spontaneously between staff, children and their families now seemed much less likely to develop unless specific plans were put into place.

Building the Key Persons approach in Example 2

There are lots of cultural sensitivities as well as professional issues we need to address here. No one should be passed over as a Key Person – that isn't fair. Just because Paula is a Rastafarian does not mean that she is not professionally competent to be a Key Person for Kamlesh. Kamlesh's parents might not choose Paula at first because she looks different to them, but we know she will do a good job in caring for children from families that are different from her own.

Things are going much better now that each Key Person has only one new child to settle in at a time. Settling in is stressful for the Key Person as well as for the child. It takes time and support from all of us. The senior management team (SMT) has staggered admissions to ensure that every child and family can go through the settling-in programme without being rushed. The SMT also needs to ensure that the new information booklet will explain this staggered admissions system to all the parents … and to grandparents too! They can put pressure on the nursery staff to admit children early when things are difficult at home.

Language and terminology

Please can we remind everyone that it is essential to be precise about the words we use and what they mean for us, for example 'key nursery groups', and not 'family groups'. We think it is important to be clear that we are not the children's family, or trying to replicate that in any way. The Key Person nursery groups in the Centre are different kinds of attachment networks from those at home.

Practical activities to 'bond' key nursery groups and their Key Person together

These are special and personal activities created by each Key Person for 'her' children and their families, for example:

- nursery group photograph albums;
- 'message boxes' for children to leave gifts, objects and toys for each other;
- coffee mornings and picnic days for key group families so that each family can get to know the others with whom they share a Key Person;
- 'gift boxes', opened at nursery group times, which contain objects from the Key Person to 'her children'; for example, autumn leaves, all of which are different but specially selected to enhance their sense of belonging to a special group;
- a collection of small purses, bags or boxes containing different things including personal things from home;
- Aziza is going back to Pakistan for a few months to mourn with her family after the death of her grandfather. We think it is important to prepare her and the others in her key group for her short absence. How shall we find rituals to say goodbye to children who are leaving the key group, or to welcome them back after an absence of some weeks? We have agreed to email her auntie in Pakistan with messages for her and her mother to keep in touch and sustain their sense of belonging to the group here.

FIGURE 3.3 Example of the discussion notes from a development team meeting (see Example 2).

Yet in contrast to the nursery group or the early years' centre examples, there is no realistic opportunity in a small private nursery to close for training or professional development days and there is certainly no Director of Quality and Training! The realities of managing a small business – ensuring financial viability and offering a reliable service to parents and secure employment to staff – places a high priority on continuity of service and maintenance of fee income. This nursery closed in the owner's home on a Friday and opened again in its new premises on the following Monday with no break of service to the children and families. Planning and thinking about closeness and continuity of relationships, therefore, had to be built in alongside an enormous variety of practical tasks.

In order to prepare the ground for this major change of size and site, but also with a determined commitment to ensuring children felt a sense of belonging and being special in the new nursery, the owner/manager began to plan for implementing a Key Persons approach. She asked her staff to read about the Key Persons approach as described by Goldschmied and Jackson (1994; 2004).

In retrospect, the owner/manager feels this was an important starting point but, as always, reading theory in a book is only the very first step in the journey of making it happen in practice. The staff members were asked to discuss the approach in a staff meeting. Finding time for staff meetings is a significant problem for small nursery businesses, which need to recover the cost of closing during working hours. Asking staff to stay on after work for staff meetings is not straightforward either.

But this nursery found an effective compromise between recognising the needs of the staff to have their evenings off, and the need for them to participate in regular professional development sessions. So it is built into contracts: all staff must attend an evening staff meeting about once every six weeks. The meeting is carefully structured with a clear agenda; discussion is professional and focused, and meetings last no longer than two hours (Figure 3.4). The staff are not paid but get a hot meal, making it a bit of a social occasion and a real model of the needs of staff being thought about as they are asked to consider the needs of the children.

In this carefully planned space for talking and thinking, some of the staff's anxieties about the Key Person role described by Goldschmied and Jackson began to emerge. Two concerns in particular were prominent and are familiar from our experience in other nurseries:

1   Being called a 'Key Person' not only raises parents' expectations of what this role might mean but also propagates the fear of not being able to fulfil it.
2   It is impossible for Key People to be with 'their key children' all of the time.

Interestingly, the owner/manager described how a few of the parents were familiar with the term 'Key Person' and responded very enthusiastically to the idea of having one for their child. Naturally, some staff became anxious about what parents might come to expect, and whether they could or should be trying to meet these expectations. This nursery had not done any preparatory work with parents and felt, with hindsight, that it would have helped to ensure that parents and staff had matching hopes, if only to reduce some of the fears about overwhelming expectations.

Challenges for the Senior Management Team (SMT) in Example 3

- Managers need to revisit the allocation of paired Key Persons (main Key Person and back-up Key Person) so as to cover annual leave, training and other reasons for absence. At present, the manager of the room is standing in as the second person. This works to some extent as she knows all the children, but it is unmanageable long term because there are days when too many children need her when their Key Person is away training or sick. It is also confusing for the children. We suggest that paired Key Persons take on that role for emotional support and group work while the manager will be a back-up for organising activities and practical tasks not directly involving the children. This means that Key Persons and their groups will move on together in the centre and that will achieve more consistency for children and Key Persons as both progress through the centre.

- We feel strongly that each member of staff should be trusted to be a Key Person and that each Key Person is inducted and trained for her special role. The Key Person role is taken by every member of staff, not only the most gregarious, or the member of staff who happens to be of a similar ethnic background to a particular family, or appears to be in tune with a particular child-rearing style. We think it is important that each Key Person is supported to take that role with her group of children, and that no one is pressurised to admit children earlier if things are difficult at home. Some families may try and pressurise us because they do not understand how we are trying to implement settling in. This is an important point for Kittan's mother and grandma, as Kittan will be joining the nursery soon. Have we translated the settling-in policy booklet into Yoruba yet?

- Please can the SMT check new admissions to accommodate part-time and full-time places. At the moment, Josie [Key Person] has too many children in her group on Wednesday morning. Tania [manager] is helping out and the ratio is OK but it is a bit hectic with so many part-time places that morning. Some of Josie's key children became distressed when she did not have time to greet them as 'individually' as on other mornings.

- There is an issue with Kamlesh. Her father wants Sakina to be her Key Person as they both speak Punjabi/Urdu. We don't think that is going to be possible at the moment – Sakina already has a full group of children with a Pakistani background. Do we really want to give parents that kind of choice? Is that in line with our equal opportunities policy? After all, we have agreed that *all* staff are entitled to professional opportunities and should have responsibilities for families from *all* kinds of minority and majority ethnic backgrounds. All Key Persons need to be trained and supported to be able to work with any family, not only the ones who may speak the same home language or practise the same religion as them. Please can we talk that through at the next staff meeting?

FIGURE 3.4 Notes from a development team meeting as staff work on refining their Key Persons approach, strengthening practice and solving problems (see Example 3).

What is the basis for the second concern on p. 50, though? As we hope we have made clear, there is no suggestion that a Key Person could or even should be with their key children all the time! Perhaps based on these anxieties, the staff chose to use the term 'special person' rather than 'Key Person', arguing that it expressed more directly what the role meant for them. Taking the trouble to ensure there is an adult who is designated 'special person' to a child has the effect of making that child feel special. This matters most of all at the beginning of the day when children arrive at nursery. For new children, particularly the youngest who are often coping with separation as a new experience, this may be the time when they most feel they are not special enough and that is why they have been left by their parents. This nursery has a policy that one member of staff is designated each day to be by the door so that every child and parent is greeted individually. This policy seemed particularly important as a platform on which to build the Key Persons approach: from being greeted by 'someone' (*any* member of the staff) to being greeted by your special person (not just *any* member of staff, but a *particular* member of staff).

Over the last year in their new premises, the Key Persons approach has grown, but with ebbs and flows. There are continual practical and logistical difficulties to solve, plus the normal human tendency to let working practices lapse. Part of the challenge of implementing the Key Persons approach is a commitment to the 'long haul'! It is a challenge of continually holding onto the importance of individual relationships when collective generalised care can be organisationally so much easier.

The Key Persons approach: documenting the role

Given what we said earlier about the anxieties many practitioners feel about making close relationships with individual children, it is very helpful for staff to have some easily readable written guidance on the essential elements of being a Key Person. In settings that have done this, it seems practitioners feel more confident individually of what is expected (and that they will not be criticised for facilitating attachments). It is then much easier to achieve a common approach amongst all staff.

One way of making the role of Key Person explicit, and we think much more manageable, is to write a 'job description' – an effective way of setting out key responsibilities and bringing into sharp focus the division between what, wherever possible, the Key Person should do, and activities that remain team responsibilities. In one nursery, a member of staff said 'We are all Key People – we all matter.' Of course this is true; the whole staff team will retain a collective responsibility for all the children in the nursery.

But nurseries should outline the specific responsibilities of the Key Person for particular children. This does not mean that team working is abandoned; rather, that team relationships are developed. It takes a considerable degree of support and trust for each member of staff to know when to hold back from responding to or doing something for a child, allowing the Key Person to fulfil this role instead. A nursery staff team might adapt the list of responsibilities listed in Figure 3.5.

Figure 3.5 contains an important list of the basic responsibilities of the Key Person role. In the case study that follows, a practitioner shows her reflection and thoughtfulness about the point 'Eating with your key children in small key groups' and how to translate this into the reality of day-to-day interactions (Randolph Beresford Centre, 1999).

Together these elements constitute a Key Persons approach

- Developing secure trusting relationships with your key children and parents.

- Interacting with your key children with reciprocal sounds, words, facial expressions and gestures, according to their individual temperament.

- Providing a secure base for your key children by supporting their interests and explorations away from you. Perhaps by smiling and nodding as they explore and by drawing their attention to interesting things around them.

- Providing a secure base for your key children by being physically and emotionally available to them to come back to, by sitting at their level and in close proximity to them.

- Using body language, eye contact and voice tone to indicate that you are available and interested, gauging these according to the child's temperament and culture.

- Understanding and containing children's difficult feelings by gentle holding, providing words for feelings and empathy in a way suited to each individual child.

- Comforting distressed children by acknowledging their feelings, offering explanations and reassurances calmly and gently.

- Acknowledging and allowing children to express a range of feelings – such as anger, joy, distress, excitement, jealousy, love.

- Settling new key children into the setting gradually.

- Settling your key children as they arrive each day.

- Eating with your key children in small key groups.

- Holding key children who are bottle-fed on your lap to feed, maintaining eye contact and conversations.

- Changing and toileting your key children, using sensitive handling and familiar words.

- Dressing and washing your key children, offering help as needed but also supporting their growing skills.

- Having regular opportunities to reflect on the emotional aspects of key working with a skilled, knowledgeable manager or colleague.

FIGURE 3.5 Important aspects of a Key Person's relationship.

Source: Manning-Morton and Thorpe 2001: section 2, p. 9.

Case study: Reflections on the Key Person role

I have thought about keeping boundaries for my Key Person role at lunchtime. I try to keep my voice calm; I try to be controlled, to be the big person, the adult for the child, to have empathy for the child. I have been reading about family relationships – that has been helpful. The book describes 'how children push the walls out to see if the roof will come down on their heads'. I try to make the walls/boundaries strong for them, so that the roof doesn't fall in, so the children feel safe with me as a strong adult.

I think mealtimes work best when the children are in a small group with their Key Person, so that they can have conversations, really talk together, not just be given instructions about what or how to eat or behave.

I am bothered about how we do that at mealtimes. Am I imposing my own ideas of good manners, or setting a pattern for conversations at mealtimes that may be very different from how things are at home for these children?

At home parents may be busy with cooking. Here Bronagh brings everything in for us, is it right that we teach our children our way (culture/family style or values), or should we think about other ways more matched to their home lives?

Mealtimes can be difficult, noisy, chaotic … that can be hard for the children. Callum likes to play under the table, Honeybee wants to push her chair in and out, their jokes together can get out of hand, too noisy for me but they are having a good time playing with one another …

Home visits and establishing a partnership

The staff of Woodlands Park Nursery Centre make it clear in their *Information for Parents* (see Figure 3.2) that the home visit is the starting point for their Key Persons approach. But they are sensitive to it being the parents' right to decide whether they want such a visit. As the starting point of a partnership between home and nursery in the care of a child, this consciousness of the dynamics of power – 'who is in charge and how are things decided', the importance of decisions being shared and being seen to be shared – seems essential in setting the pattern of how decisions will be collectively made and information exchanged as the child's career in nursery continues.

In private nurseries, this relationship can seem quite different to that experienced with a local authority centre. Having a 'customer orientation' is good business practice in any enterprise. When the business is a nursery and the customer is the parent, the power relationship between parent and nursery is likely to shift from 'Will this nursery want to give my child a place?' to 'Will this parent want to buy a place in my nursery?' Understandably, in the latter case, nursery staff may be afraid to talk about home visits or a settling-in process in case these are seen by the parents as unnecessary or inconvenient and lead to the parent going elsewhere. The reality of a shortage of places may make this unlikely although demand varies. The staff of private nurseries, however, need the clear support of managers and owners to negotiate and plan a partnership between nursery and home where the child remains clearly in focus as a 'customer' too.

FIGURE 3.6 A Key Person in the nursery sharing a book with a child. Both of them are facing the pages together and sharing the experiences that they have together been a part of, or that have been related by the child's parents. The adult makes connections with the past experiences so that the child can make sense of new ones.

The benefits, and potential for partnership, of the home visit seem more than evident in the following parent's description of her child starting at a nursery in the London Borough of Camden:

When we had our home visit I explained how Liam loves pottering round the flat trailing anything with a flex behind him, like the vacuum cleaner or my hair dryer. On his first day Leon [the nursery worker] had put out lengths of string tied to little toys and, in the garden, there were lengths of garden hose. I was amazed, and touched, at the care and interest he'd taken.

(Manning-Morton and Thorpe, 2001: section 8, p. 3)

Building a key group

This has been one of the most difficult parts of the book to write. Should the linking of new children to the nursery with a particular Key Person, and building the key group of children for whom a Key Person is responsible, be largely a matter of 'who clicks with who' or should it be a more definitely managed and directed activity?

Sometimes children or parents make spontaneous links with a particular member of staff in nursery (perhaps the member of staff who showed them around when they first visited the setting). It may then seem 'natural' that this member of staff should become the Key Person for that child and his or her family. There may be scope to take into account such 'linking' in allocating children to a particular Key Person.

We would argue, however, that to allow this to be the main allocation system in the nursery would undermine the need for the Key Persons approach to be integrated into the nursery's overall management arrangements. We make some general points here about building the key group. In the next chapter, we say more about building key groups with 3- and 4-year-olds.

The role of Key Person needs to be a proactive one. A central part of the role of being a Key Person is to get to know a family, ask parents and carers to share information about home life and background and to learn about the religious, linguistic and cultural background of the family. The very concept of a 'Key Person' may be unfamiliar in some cultures. A Chinese parent, while receptive to the provision of a special relationship in the setting between a Key Person and her child, could not relate this to her own experience of relationships with professionals in her part of China. In the English nursery her child attended, the Key Person was able to find out about the different values and priorities of early years provision in China and be more sensitive to this parent's background and expectations.

There may be some preexisting relationship between the family and a member of staff in the setting. However, we are concerned that the idea of decisions about which practitioner should be Key Person for which child and family being made on this basis is not a good approach. We think it denies, or certainly underplays, the central management function of balancing the overall intake of children to the setting and positive, managed allocation. By this we mean ensuring each child is allocated to a Key Person, taking active account of the size of that Key Person's existing group of children and of that person's availability to settle a new child (for example, have they just embarked on settling another child? Are they about to go on holiday?).

In one setting, the manager allocates all children to an established member of staff (new members of staff are given time to manage their own settling in before being asked to help children with settling in). But the matching process, undertaken by the deputy managers (involved in day-to-day dealings with the children and more likely to have a clearer insight into the children's individual needs than the manager), is logistically complex.

One basic consideration is the need to ensure, as far as possible, that part-time staff are linked to children who attend nursery on corresponding days. Existing members of staff should not be allocated too many children; for the role of Key Person to remain viable, the maximum number is perhaps five or six.

Another consideration is the timing of admissions. Local authority and LEA-maintained settings may be able to delay admitting children until the appropriate Key Person is available to help them settle (see Example 2, above). For settings that have to perform very tight financial balancing acts, delaying admissions may not be commercially possible. However, a settling-in plan centred on judgements about the child's needs should as far as possible be the first priority.

One setting starts the Key Person relationship with a two-week settling-in period. The first week, the parent stays with their child. The Key Person concentrates on getting to know the child and family and aims to help them become familiar with the nursery. During the second week, parent and Key Person can begin to plan graduated times for leaving the child. It is so easy to underestimate the sophistication of this professional work by the Key Person. She will draw on her knowledge and training as well as on her personal experience of coping with partings and reunions. And parents have widely differing feelings and ways of coping with the intrinsic difficulty of handing the care of their child to someone else. They have different external demands too and some will be under much greater pressure than others to hurry through this period. While parents and the Key Person often start to build a powerful bond during this time, they will not always be comfortable partners or 'of one mind' about how to manage the details of this settling-in process.

One parent complained that her designated Key Person was not often available to speak to her. When the manager raised this with the practitioner, she explained how intimidating she found the parent and recognised that, while she was working very closely with the child, she did tend to avoid the parent.

How does a manager respond to this basic block to building an effective partnership? She has to make a judgement about whether this is a difficulty that she can help the member of staff manage, as part of the staff member's own growth and development, or whether that is unrealistic at that particular time. On this occasion, the manager decided to switch Key Persons while being careful to make it a learning rather than a negative experience for the staff member concerned.

We believe this Key Person 'switching' should be very much a last resort. If the Key Persons approach is to be understood as a way of building close professional relationships between the worker, child and family, this must be recognised as a sophisticated task that will entail challenges and uncertainties, as well as learning new skills of interacting with parents – parents whose social or cultural background may differ greatly from the Key Person's. The professional development of the Key Person depends on these challenges being addressed and worked at. Changing the Key Person may limit the opportunity for this professional development to take place.

The intimidation can work the other way too. Another parent was visibly anxious about being in the nursery. Yet the link between her and her child's Key Person has proved immensely positive. When the Key Person commented on how much the child had grown in confidence, his mother commented 'I have too!' We should not underestimate the potential benefits that a successful Key Person relationship can bring to the whole family.

Observing, noticing and not noticing

What helps or hinders how much detail Key Persons can observe or notice about the children for whom they are responsible? During a seminar discussion, a nursery manager described how difficult it was to staff her baby unit:

> Some of the girls say it is boring working with the babies – it's not like the 3- and 4-year-olds; babies don't do much and the day passes so slowly.

When there is so much to notice and observe in the rapid growth and development of the first months and years, how can it be that babies might be perceived as uninteresting to the point of being boring? Parents and close relatives take such obvious delight in their baby's new gestures, facial expressions or vocalisation. Why then is this not mirrored by the experience of staff in baby rooms?

There are of course the practical factors of time and how busy staff are that will affect anyone's capacity to observe or notice the details of interactions and development. However, we think that another important factor is that staff may sometimes 'distance themselves' from individual babies and young children in favour of generalised attention to the group precisely because very young children can be so individually engaging. Young children have and need a powerful capacity to engage adults, evoking pleasure and delight. Working effectively with a baby or young child means involvement, being drawn into a relationship and responding to the child. Connection and affection cannot grow without the risk of pain and loss when the baby or toddler, inevitably, moves on. So staff may avoid this involvement by not allowing themselves to notice babies' or young children's overtures and interactions.

There is a second reason for 'not noticing'. While much of what a baby or young child communicates may be obvious and delightful, the opposite also applies. The meaning of a baby's piercing cries or expressions of bewilderment may take time to interpret – what precisely is it that is so upsetting to the baby? It is completely understandable to want to stop this distress. The sometimes frantic efforts of nursery practitioners to distract babies and young children from their feelings by jiggling them up and down or showing them toys or mobiles are good examples of an inability to notice and think about what is really being communicated. The primary goal seems to be to stop the communication rather than understand it. The challenge of detailed 'noticing' is described by Margaret Rustin:

to be a good observer ... requires a space in the mind where thoughts can begin to take shape and where confused experiences can be held in an inchoate (disorganised or confused) form until their meaning becomes clearer. This kind of mental functioning requires a capacity to tolerate anxiety, uncertainty, discomfort, helplessness, a sense of bombardment.

(Rustin, 1989: 20–1)

When given 'permission' to begin to observe in this way, to record impressions and personal feelings without being immediately clear about their meaning or significance, practitioners expressed their delight at how much there was to see (Shropshire and Telford and Wrekin Early Years and Child Care Development Partnership, 2000). The simple acknowledgement that practitioners do have feelings about what they do and what they see appears to remove some of the fear, allowing them to notice more.

This type of detailed observation requires concentration and cannot be done while working alongside the children. Some nurseries have managed this by allowing a staff member working in one room to observe in another, perhaps for a 20-minute 'block' during the day. Other settings have released staff to take turns to observe within a team, an example of which is the Avranches Nursery Professional Development Sessions, which were held in 1999–2000 in Jersey, Channel Islands.

However it is organised, the Key Persons approach in action must be monitored and informed by focused, detailed, individual child observations.

Sharing and not sharing information

The Key Persons approach makes it possible for carers to bring informed and detailed knowledge of a child to the discussion of observation material and to make the best sense of it.

When parents in one nursery were asked to share something significant about what their children did at nursery that day, some said that they did not know, but added that, in some ways, they felt they *could not really expect to know* (Elfer, 2008). They explain that having made the choice to place their child in nursery, inevitably, at least in part, they had to give up on that detailed knowledge of what their child did each day. It was as if the parents felt they could not have the best of both worlds – that is, having a job *and* knowing what their child was doing.

Why should parents feel excluded or exclude themselves in this way? Certainly there was no suggestion that the nurseries had been reluctant to share information. But the parents' *perception* that they were not really entitled to it does highlight the role of the Key Person in taking the initiative to build a positive relationship, to offer information and to make clear the nursery's need for information from home. Taking a passive role and waiting for parents to ask will not be enough for some parents.

Where the Key Person is not on duty when parents arrive to collect their child, nurseries sometimes use very simple devices to pass on information: 'Please remember to tell Daniel's parents that today, he did X and Y.' Liam's parent (see p. 56) was touched (and presumably reassured about the nursery's commitment to take note of the information she had passed on in the home visit) by the trouble Leon had gone

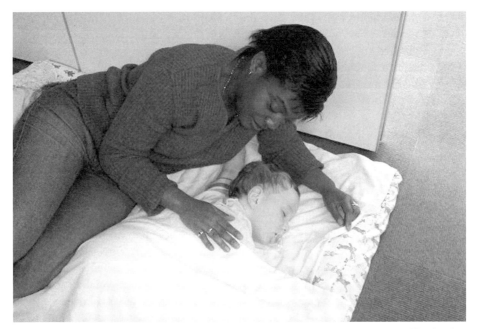

FIGURE 3.7 The Key Person settles the child to sleep. She pats him gently on his back. This is what his mother says he needs in order to drift off to sleep. With his hand he rubs the Key Person's woolly jumper and he sucks gently on his dummy – both comforting sensations that help him feel safe enough to sleep.

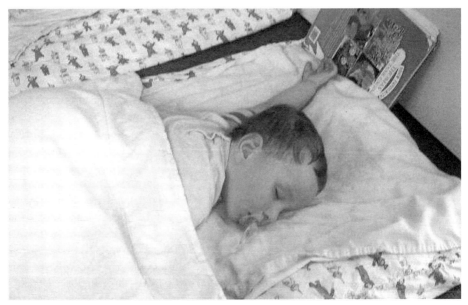

FIGURE 3.8 Once the child is settled and sleeping, the Key Person leaves his favourite storybook close by for when he awakes. The child is lying on his own special blanket from home so that the smells and associations of home may comfort and calm him.

to on Liam's behalf. A parent is likely to be similarly touched by the trouble taken to remind a colleague to pass on some detail of what Daniel had done. This personalised exchange of information is very important. Some settings have developed standardised proformas to help ensure all parents do receive consistent sets of daily feedback. This can be formulaic, however; sometimes, little more than records of inputs (food and drink) and outputs (nappy changes). It is no substitute for the personalised, individual feedback that only the Key Person or her back-up can provide.

Discussion in professional teams reveals the dilemmas of what *not* to tell parents. The following is a typical piece of advice:

> When a child takes her first step, it's better to tell parents, 'She looks as though she is about to take her first step so look out for it at home.' When they come to you in a week's time and say, 'You were right, she has just taken her first step' you let them enjoy that privilege and do not say, 'Oh we saw that two weeks ago.'

This seems very sensitive, well-intentioned practice. But is it consistent with an honest and open relationship with parents? Or does it treat parents as if they are very vulnerable and have to be protected from what they probably know already?

Aspect 4: Who is the 'Key Person' for the Key Person? Mentoring and professional supervision

This fourth element of making the Key Persons approach a reality in practice concerns the support each Key Person needs in order to be effective.

The Key Persons approach does make all professional relationships closer and more interactive – with children, with parents and family members and with colleagues. It would be irresponsible to allow, never mind encourage, these more complex relationships to be fostered without a system of checks and balances to ensure that professional boundaries are maintained and that practice is clearly accountable within the early years management system. We do not believe the Key Person role can be done well (or perhaps done at all) unless the inherent emotional demands and accountability that goes with it, are acknowledged and addressed.

The challenge of emotionally close relationships with children

Encouraging individually distinct relationships in early years settings means professionals have to cope with their own painful feelings of change and loss. A little boy wanted to 'move away' from his Key Person in order to spend more time exploring and being with other adults and children. The Key Person was hurt: 'He doesn't love or need me any more.' The head of the setting felt she had to try to understand and discuss the practitioner's feelings rather than label her as 'unprofessional' or 'possessive'. Another child, having become confident and independent, regressed when his baby sister was born, returning to a stage of wanting greater closeness to and attention from his Key Person. His Key Person understood what was happening and responded positively.

Feeling hurt by children's 'rejections' as they express their preference for particular staff or assert their independence is not restricted to junior staff or those who are inexperienced. In this quotation, the practitioner was a highly trained and very experienced professional:

> when Alison (2) first started she'd just give me the most appalling looks and I said 'Kim, Alison doesn't like me', and she's like, 'Don't take it personally', and I said, 'No I never would, I couldn't afford to in this job …'. But as soon as Kim came in, Alison would be, 'Oh Kim', and her whole face would light up and I'd be 'Oh God Alison doesn't love me', and we'd have this laugh between us all. When Kim was away, Alison would sort of come closer … she let me put her down in her cot, but she screamed blue murder initially. She'd be like 'aaaah!' Kim would go in and she'd stop.
>
> (Elfer, 2008)

Sometimes, this description of the practitioner's reaction to Alison's preference for Kim has prompted criticism and suggestions that perhaps the person is in the wrong job! Yet, observations in the setting showed the sophistication and professionalism of her interactions with children. We think the member of staff was being honest in her description of her feelings and professional in discussing them with her colleagues. In this way, she was able to ensure that, when working with the children, she could continue to work in a professional way, setting her ordinary feelings of rejection to one side knowing that her colleagues had heard them and understood them, and did not criticise or judge her for having these feelings.

What about parents? How do they respond to these obviously important relationships their children make with other adults? In one way, their responses and reactions are as variable as those of the staff. Most parents seem to be relieved that there is a 'special person' for them and their child. However, Page and Nutbrown (2008: 181–7) have shown how some parents may feel threatened and anxious. Parents then need time and support from a senior practitioner in the setting to help them understand that the Key Person is not there to take over their central role as parent but rather to help the child feel secure whilst at the setting.

The challenge of physically close relationships with children

On top of the inherent but ordinary complexity of close human relationships, close relationships with young children in early years settings are complex because of the child protection issues involved.

Babies and young children need holding, cuddling and lap time, all of which are the very essence of being in a relationship. The Key Persons approach maximises this in so far as it incorporates more physical contact conducted mainly by the same adults, but always arising out of the child's, rather than the adult's, needs.

It would be irresponsible to ignore the dangers of physical and sexual abuse. Thankfully, the number of documented incidents in early years settings is small but the deep and long-lasting damage wreaked by abuse of any kind places a great responsibility on every practitioner and manager to be alert and sensitive to any evidence of inappropriate contact.

Some local authorities are developing policies to guide practitioners – an important step in ensuring that children are protected from inappropriate contact, as well as from inadequate physical contact. We've often heard practitioners say, 'Of course you're not allowed contact with children any more – it's "child protection"'. Denying children physical comforting and holding would be as abusive to youngsters as imposing it for adults' gratification. So it is really important to check out exactly what the 'child protection' policies of the setting, organisation or local authority do actually say and what they do not say.

Many local authority policies seem to have struck a sensitive balance in placing physical touch at the centre of the 'curriculum' for the youngest children. Figure 3.9 provides a good example of this from St Stephen's Nursery Centre in East London.

It is important for children to see practitioners interacting and relating to each other in positive ways. In this nursery we positively encourage the staff and children to develop happy, secure relations and play together. Our teaching through play policy includes the area of emotional development. The following details the ways in which personal relationships between adults/children are developed:

- through physical contact, such as holding children's hands;

- holding children gently to reassure them;

- cuddling children to express delight in their behaviour;

- tickling them, to gain attention, to respond to their attempts at communication;

- laughing with children when they show excitement, discovery and pleasure in the world;

- smiling, making funny faces;

- sitting children on your lap, giving comfort to them when they are upset and helping them to achieve a goal;

- talking about things that can make children and adults happy or sad.

FIGURE 3.9 Example of nursery guidelines on physical touch and holding.

People sometimes object to men taking on the role of Key Person. But some early years settings have taken a very positive approach not only to the need for more men to be working as early childhood professionals, but also for them to take a full part in the care of the youngest children:

Parents have at various times expressed misgivings about men giving intimate care (nappy changing, toileting children etc.) and also put forward more general objections based on ideas of men taking away women's power by moving into the work. These objections have been met by establishing and publicising a witnessing policy, whereby workers do not give intimate care alone but work together, and by pointing out to the parents that if gender equality is achieved it will be because each gender is willing to give up its area of sole control. Some exceptions have been made in the area of intimate care for some parents – almost invariably for cultural or religious reasons.

(Bateman, 1998: 164)

It is important that protection strategies for *all* staff in settings and schools are developed. We need to keep in mind that a mixed gender workforce in early years has many benefits for a child, her family and for the Key Persons in the staff team. It is paramount that appropriate physical closeness is encouraged for both male and female Key Persons. As Cameron *et al.* (1999: 173) advocate, we should separate the perceived link between male childcare workers and sexual abuse of children. What is more important is that we develop reflexive practice and consensual policies to protect children and the men and women who interact and relate to children within the professional boundaries of the Key Person's role.

An early years policy on physical contact as set out in Figure 3.9, perhaps within the context of a wider philosophy as set out in the extract above, needs to be part of the 'infrastructure' of building the Key Persons approach.

The challenge of close relationships with parents and other family members

It is often said that to hand over one's child into the care of others, particularly to others who may be almost strangers as in the case of a child attending an early years setting for the first time, is one of the most difficult things for a parent to do. Parents may spend anxious weeks and months, as the time to return to work after a period of maternity leave approaches. Perhaps they will be thinking about types of childcare and visiting different settings. As deadlines approach and options narrow down, parents may feel an odd mixture of intensifying anxiety and possible relief as the period of agonising draws to a close and a decision must be made.

We know from conversations with many professionals in early years settings that it can seem exactly like this as they show parents around and get to know new parents who have chosen to send their child to the setting. We know that it can seem very different too with parents seeming sometimes casual, as if any setting 'will do', and wishing to rush through or avoid altogether any settling in period. As we pointed out on p. 35, it is important to keep in mind that this may be a way of parents protecting themselves from the painful feelings of trusting someone else. It may also be a more straightforward expression of parents' relief that a setting they can afford and trust has at last been found. Many parents are under immense pressure in managing the complexities of paid employment, family life and making financial ends meet and may have other children to worry about too.

Whether parents 'click' with the practitioners in a setting immediately, whether it takes a little longer, or whether a settled, trusting relationship always seems slightly out of reach, the point we are making is that this partnership between home and setting is an immensely sensitive one but also an immensely significant one. If you turn back to the example we gave in Chapter 1 of Melissa and her mother's fury, perhaps masking terror, at Lilia, Melissa's Key Person, and the attachment Melissa had formed to Lilia, you can see the sensitive tightrope that practitioners sometimes have to walk:

> Do your best not to compete with parents. When two or more people take care of one child there's bound to be some rivalry, sometimes; it even happens within families, between parents, say or between a parent and a grandparent. Try not to join in a 'who does he love the best?' competition, though. If a child is to get the best out of the care you and his parents share, you have to feel able to work closely with them – and sometimes, with some parents, that is surprisingly difficult. Parents want children to be happy in childcare – but perhaps not too happy. Although a mother is probably grateful and flattered that you love her baby or toddler, that won't stop her worrying privately about how much the baby or toddler loves you. And of course, come the inevitable day when a tired, balky 1-year-old doesn't want to leave at going home time, the mother (who is probably overtired herself) is all set to decide that you've stolen her prime place in her child's affections.
>
> (Leach, 2008: 21–8)

We have already said earlier in this chapter (see *Sharing and not sharing information* on p. 59) that staff may be anxious about what feedback to give to parents concerning their child's day, not wanting parents to 'miss out'. A practitioner put it like this to us, 'if a parent has been away from their child all day, you don't want to go and twist the knife by excitedly telling her all the brilliant things her child has done during the day – have a heart!' Some parents have told us that they would really value this kind of sensitivity and do not want to be told what their child has done because it would be difficult for them to be confronted with how much they may have missed seeing for themselves. However, other parents have told us that of course they *do* want to know what their child has done, that they know as parents that the early years setting will see many 'firsts' but they do not want to be kept in the dark.

How do practitioners manage this? It seems to us another reason why the Key Persons role is so important. It is only by building a close relationship between the family and *someone*, not *anyone*, in the setting, that the sensitive conversation about what information parents would like the practitioners to provide can develop. Parents will have different feelings and in the end, it is only by raising questions like this that a shared decision can be made and a strong partnership can be built. Practitioners may sometimes feel anxious about upsetting parents, especially in private settings, where there is not only the professional partnership relationship to be considered but the realities of a customer relationship too. Here, it is perhaps helpful to keep in mind Sue Greenfields' research pointing out the complexities of partnership relationships and how anxious parents can feel about teachers, and probably other early years professionals too, in the context of home visiting:

> The teachers did not at any time indicate they were aware that they held the power in their relationship with parents and yet there is evidence of the teachers' influence over the parents … There was no choice about the time of the visits or

whether a visit should take place at all. In some settings there were policies to compel parents to agree to a home visit otherwise their child would be unable to attend the setting. The only way that parents could get out of the visit was by being out of the house at the time of the appointment.

(Greenfield, forthcoming)

We are very aware of many teachers who work hard to be sensitive to the power dynamics in their relationships with families but Greenfield's research reminds us of the difficulties that can occur. We finish this section on the complexity of partnership relationships with parents wishing to emphasise the need for practitioners to have training and support in managing them but also to re state their huge value. As Barnes *et al.* conclude, strong relationships with parents may be of huge value in helping mothers:

Bringing their own feelings into the open and having them acknowledged as legitimate may enable them to deal more effectively with the child care once it begins. These findings also highlight the importance of training caregivers to understand their professional role with parents as well as with children and supporting them as they undertake both together.

(Barnes *et al.*, 2006)

FIGURE 3.10 A nursery Key Person having support and supervision. The nursery manager plans in regular times when staff with responsibilities for particular children have time to talk, so as to develop their work with the children and their families. The supervisor also introduces the Key Person to relevant reading material to support her professional development.

Mentoring and supervision: the practice and some examples

We want to emphasise that we do not think only junior or inexperienced staff need mentoring and supervision. We think it should be an essential and integral part of the practice of all early years professionals, however well qualified and experienced. Margy Whalley (1996: 170) has highlighted the importance of supervision in early years settings:

> It would not have been possible for staff to remain open to criticism and to appraise their own work critically if they had not received consistent supervision. We set up a system where most staff receive supervision/support every three weeks from a senior member of staff. Senior staff then receive support from the Head of Centre who in turn has a monthly consultancy session with an external consultant (a lecturer in the University social work department). This level of supervision is essential for staff working in a centre for under-fives which combines a social work and educative role working as a team.

This importance of a forum for thinking about the emotional impact of work inter-actions is now also being accepted in some schools with teachers (Jackson, 2008) as well as in early years settings (Elfer and Dearnley, 2007). The aim is to support staff:

- Think about the ways in which children's states of mind can impact at an emotional level on staff and the culture and ethos of the early years setting and vice versa.

- Explore ways in which adverse past experiences for staff and children can affect future relationships and experiences.

- Increase awareness of how groups and teams may operate 'below the surface' and lead to a powerful sense for members of those teams about whether difficulties and uncertainties can be discussed, without criticism or blame, or the opposite, a place where you keep problems to yourself, where to put your 'head above the parapet' feels too risky.

These supervision and mentoring sessions, whether one-to-one or in groups, are *not* therapy! They are not places to discuss (or probe) private issues and feelings. They are about establishing relationships of trust in order to facilitate critical reflection about the impact of emotion on work and work interactions (Elfer and Dearnley, 2007: 267–79).

An example of why such regular and systematic review is necessary is given in the following case study.

Case study: Keeping professional boundaries accountable and under review

'Beginnings' is a private nursery in a rural part of the Midlands. The nursery has been developing its Key Persons approach for a year and each member of staff has responsibility for a small group of children of mixed ages. One of Kevin's key children is Jack who is 18 months. Jack arrived in nursery one morning apparently quite well but, by lunchtime, staff were concerned that he appeared unwell, and when they took his temperature it was nearly 100°F. Kevin phoned Jack's mother and she agreed to leave work and collect Jack. When she arrived nearly an hour later, Jack's temperature had gone up a little further. Jack seemed pleased and relieved to see his mother and she took him home, saying she might take Jack to the doctor. During the remainder of his shift, Kevin phoned Jack's mother twice to see how he was. He also phoned from home in the evening to see what the doctor had said. Next day, Jack's mother asked to speak to the nursery manager. She said she did not want to seem unappreciative of the care Kevin had taken but she felt his phone call the previous evening had been a 'bit over the top'. She felt her care of Jack was being checked up on.

It does seem as if Kevin has allowed his professional relationship with Jack and Jack's parents to become blurred, and that while his phone calls may have been very well intentioned, Jack's mother experienced them as inappropriate and intrusive. It is a good example of why we emphasise that it would be irresponsible to implement a Key Persons approach without the checks and monitoring provided by a supervision and mentoring system.

Some early years settings are already implementing a mentoring system effectively while others are beginning to build it into nursery budgets as an essential cost. We give three examples below of how this is happening in practice. First, Helen Watson (2002; personal communication with authors) describes, from a practitioner's point of view, just how integral the mentoring and supervision process is considered to be within an early years family centre.

Case study: Supervision and mentoring

I wasn't familiar with supervision until I came to work at Netherton Park Family Centre as a seconded deputy. Previously I'd worked as an early years coordinator in a school in a very challenging area of Birmingham where there was a desperate – and unmet – need for the opportunity to reflect on children and issues of concern in *regular*, carefully managed, confidential and professional meetings. At Netherton Park, members of the staff team (secretaries, nursery nurses, teachers, students, project manager and deputies) have, at least, a monthly two-hour meeting with their line manager. This is seen as so valuable that nothing is allowed to compromise it – in the rare circumstances that a meeting has to be cancelled it is immediately rescheduled.

Although certain aspects, like a discussion of children who are on either the Special Needs Register or the Child Protection register, form part of every month's agenda, there is also scope to focus on areas identified by either the worker or the line manager. We use this forum to look at issues like relationships with other staff members, children and parents, areas for development and, if needed, it's the opportunity to have a good grumble about anything and everything to do with work.

The supervisors are carefully trained in a range of supervision and counselling techniques and there is a negotiated contract (including a complaints procedure). Because of its obvious impact on self-esteem and sense of personal worth, the process plays a vital part in the good working relationships between staff, parents and children and it can have a therapeutic role. For example, in supervision recently it allowed us to reach some understanding of a parent of a child who was born with quite complex needs. The mother found it very difficult to cope with her child's growing independence and she clearly experienced jealousy of staff at the centre for the part they played in developing the child's skills. Supervision helped the child's key worker, who was understandably upset at the occasional hostile outbreaks of the parent, to put it into some framework and not to take it personally whilst developing strategies to communicate with the family.

We also have group supervisions – which we try to have off-site – where all staff involved in the nursery part of the Family Centre have an opportunity to discuss a range of common issues and to share useful information. These are very honest discussions and there appears to be little that would come under the heading of a 'no-go area'.

Supervision (which should not be confused with appraisal or staff meeting) in my experience has a wholly positive effect on the well-being of the team. In turn, this impacts on the life of the Centre and the relationships we have with children and parents.

In the next example, Chris Lewis, Head of a Nursery School in Tower Hamlets, describes her 'Talking about children meeting'.

Case study: Talking about children meeting

Children's House Nursery School is a 95-place nursery catering for 3- and 4-year-olds. There are 45 full-time places and 50 part-time places. Demand for places is high and there is a lengthy waiting list. The school was rated 'outstanding' by Ofsted at the most recent inspection (November, 2010), which stated that all staff do an outstanding job working in partnership and engaging parents in their children's learning. Inspectors also commented on the outstanding care, guidance and support offered to the children and the support offered to staff.

The school is at the heart of the local community in a deprived area of East London. Stay and play sessions are held for parents and under-3s in the afternoon, so many children are familiar with the school before taking up their nursery place.

The majority of the children are of Bangladeshi Heritage; African, Turkish, Chinese, Japanese and Pakistani are the other ethnic groups represented.

Every Wednesday we have a 'Talking about children meeting'. This is the time we set aside to support each other in our work with families and when we think together about the needs of the child and any additional needs that family may have. This weekly meeting provides staff with an opportunity to discuss their role as a Key Person and to seek support and advice from colleagues. The children are discussed on a rota and in the week preceding the meeting the Key Person will chat with the child and the parent and the child will be the focus of more intense observations.

At these meetings any difficulties that have arisen are discussed and staff think together about the way forward. We work in partnership with a wide range of agencies and following from these meetings we can refer to other professionals or signpost to other services as needed.

For example, it could be that the parent is difficult to engage with and we can refer to our parent support partner, or it may be the Key Person has had a difficulty forming a relationship with the child, or it could just be a time to think together about the next steps for that child and family.

In a way it is the closest to supervision that we can offer as each Key Person has a chance every week to discuss any difficulties and equally to celebrate successes. The meetings last 90 minutes and staff work in groups of four to six, with a senior manager attending each one.

We have found that these meetings really do provide staff with an opportunity to gain support as the role of the Key Person has a different meaning for every child and family.

And in our last example, Ann Thurgood, Head of First Steps Children's Centre in Bath, describes the support they give to staff.

Case study: Supporting staff with some of the emotional demands of the Key Person role in First Steps Children's Centre

All staff have monthly supervision sessions when there is always an opportunity to discuss the needs of the children and the pressures attached. We recognise, however, that staff can need support at the time an incident or discussion happens, rather than to fit in conveniently with these sessions. Both the assistant manager and I try therefore to be available to staff as freely as possible. If a staff member wants to talk something through and, if it is not possible to respond instantly, we ensure there is an opportunity on the day of the request. We also try to anticipate occasions that could be particularly difficult to staff, such as review, safeguarding strategy and child protection planning meetings. In this case we ask staff to report back to us as soon as possible after the meeting, asking them to update us on the result of the meeting. This then provides a natural opportunity to give any appropriate emotional support. We also take time during staff meetings for all staff to reflect on particular children and families.

Practice example

V first came to us when she was approximately 14 months old. She was living in the care of her mother who told us that she did not get on with her own mother who was very controlling. She did not have any contact with her and under no circumstances were we to have any communication with her. This of course we respected.

V settled in well in our under-2 room and built a very good relationship with her Key Person. At the beginning, mum was very chatty, talking to the Key Person about her (very ambitious) plans for the future and we were beginning to discuss her need for adult company and how we could help with this (she was not interested in Stay and Play groups).

One day we had a phone call from V's grandmother to tell us that mum had been taken into hospital and sectioned, and therefore she was now looking after V. We could not, of course, just accept this story so contacted social services to verify the truth. Once all was confirmed we then focused on the impact of this sudden change for V. Her mother had 'disappeared' and she was now being cared for by someone that she had not had any contact with for over a year, so was a stranger as far as she was concerned. The Key Person and I met with the grandmother to discuss the support we could offer. She was in a position to be able to pay for nursery fees and in fact decided that it would be very helpful to increase the amount of time that she attended. We all thought this was very positive as the Key Person was the one stable relationship in V's life.

As staff, we were also conscious of the impact that the situation was having on grandmother's life. She was very committed to helping her daughter and granddaughter, but was having to attend meetings with the hospital, social services, etc. almost on a daily basis. She had recently retired, had taken up golf and joined a couple of other classes but had to stop these because she had no time for them any longer. As well as coping with the practical issues this created, she was also having to come to terms with a huge change in her expectations for her retirement. The Key Person was again someone who she was seeing frequently and who was able to give time to listen to her.

V then reached her second birthday. We would have considered keeping her in the under-2 room but thought she needed the stimulation of being with her peers, and we had a new child booked to take up her place. The implication of this was that she would have a new Key Person from the over-3s room. It was purely by chance that another staff member from the over-3s room left at that time and so we moved V's Key Person into that room. It was fortunate that she had no preference which room she worked in. We also thought it would not have a massive impact on her other key children as they were all in stable home situations and therefore continuity for V should take priority.

Very gradually the mother's health is improving and she is now living at home with grandmother and her daughter. This means, however, that V has to accept and build a renewed relationship with her mother – someone who has 'let her down' by suddenly 'disappearing' from her day-to-day life. Again the relationship with the Key Person is vitally important.

In each of the above examples, the writer describes the particular space she has been able to create for discussions about children. What makes us think that these examples are so valuable is that they are examples of facing and discussing 'difficulties' as an ordinary and expected part of the daily work of the setting. By the term 'space', we mean two things. First we mean space in the sense of time where a group of staff can come together. We know this is difficult in settings where teams of staff, themselves needing to finely balance work and family commitments, are usually managing heavy workloads and certainly do not have time to spare. But we mean 'space' in the sense of an atmosphere or climate in which difficulties can be faced as well as successes, and achievements celebrated.

The issue is whether a space for discussion can be created and led by an experience facilitator where difficulties can be thought about together without practitioners being critical or judgemental (although there may need to be 'judgement') of each other, and without blaming those outside the setting (parents, advisers, Ofsted, the LEA, government). Those outside a setting do of course influence what happens inside the setting and there needs to be a realistic assessment of their influence. But the challenge is to avoid them becoming a 'scapegoat' in order to deflect thinking from what is happening inside the setting.

It is in order to have and maintain this type of space, something that needs building up and developing over time, that we think the 'open door' policies of some heads and managers may not be enough.

Why 'My door is always open' may not be enough

Most heads and managers we have spoken with have been very sensitive to this need in their staff and concerned to be available for support. They often say things like, 'I try to ensure my door is always open.' Given the pressures of workload and time that most heads and managers are under, this is very generous and unless senior staff are given more time to manage, it may be unreasonable to expect more. However, we know that sometimes the practitioner's response to 'My door is always open' is a mixed one of part gratitude but also part anxiety. The message may be misunderstood as really meaning 'If you can't cope, you can come and see me.' Some staff will find it very difficult to acknowledge they are struggling or are worried about a relationship with a child and family and so remain quiet.

On the other hand, if the setting is able to reserve regular time for talking only about relationships with children and families (not administrative matters), this conveys the message of expectation that this complex, deeply professional/deeply personal work does need regular attention and support – to experience difficult feelings or uncertainties or anxieties is normal, not a sign of failing to cope.

A supervision system should be seen as essential, in *every* early years setting. This is first and foremost to ensure professional boundaries are retained and that all relationships are accountable within the quality assurance processes of the nursery. But second, staff have a right and entitlement to this regular and trained support in recognition of the complex and sophisticated work they are asked to do with children and families.

The Key Persons approach for 3- to 5-year-olds

Sarah Hall is a teacher at Stockham Primary School in Oxfordshire. We introduced her description of the Key Persons approach in Chapter 2. This is an excerpt from an email message to thank her advisory teacher Amanda Slater for her training and support on introducing the Key Persons approach (2008–9).

> I can't believe how amazingly the Key Persons approach has developed in our class over the past two years … At the risk of sounding a bit obsessed with it – this year has been particularly great. The children, parents and staff all had such good working relationships this year … It really, really makes such a HUGE difference and I'm sure the way the staff have developed our Key Persons approach this year is the real basis of why this cohort achieved so well with EYFSP. Of course I'm not taking credit away from the children themselves, who were a particularly lovely and hard-working bunch. But I am actually convinced it is the most important thing for the children to feel safe, secure, valued and happy in order for learning to take place. That's why we are taking it into Year One next year – in a slightly reduced format.

Introduction

This chapter is not so much updated from the first edition of this book, but is rather another new stage on a journey of the theory and practice of a Key Persons approach. It has been written by Dorothy and Peter, without, of course, Elinor's input. Yet this new addition to the book is built on the firm foundations of the relationship we had with our mentor and Key Person, Elinor Goldschmied. We now take her work with babies and children under 3 into a new time with a new age group. Her wisdom and kindness, her attention to detail and her legacy of knowledge are ever in our minds.

Such is the legacy of our special relationship, one that was both a professional partnership but also a personal one as a friend with whom we shared so many experiences. Her films, her professional partnership with us and colleagues in the UK as well as in Europe have influenced what we write here. At the launch of the Italian version of the first edition of this book in October 2010, Professor Barbara Ongari of Trento University spoke of Elinor's lasting influence, as a teacher, mentor and friend on her and colleagues working in early childhood settings in Northern Italy.

Defining some of the terms we use

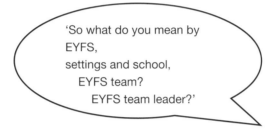

'So what do you mean by EYFS, settings and school, EYFS team? EYFS team leader?'

This chapter applies to all the Early Years Foundation Stage (EYFS) settings where children aged 3 to 5 are together in groups or classes. This will include children's centres, nursery schools and classes, voluntary pre-schools, independent schools and kindergartens, as well as children in the reception class and foundation stage units of primary schools. In this chapter, when we are including all these places we refer to them as 'settings and schools'. That is, children and staff in primary schools as well as those in all the settings before they enter school.

However, in some instances we have singled out primary schools and reception classes for discussion and guidance on the Key Persons approach. This is because this approach is a matter not only for the children and staff in the final year of the EYFS but because it is a whole school issue. It is not only relevant for the reception class teacher(s) and teaching assistant(s) but a consideration for whole school policy, management, training and practice. The EYFS team in the reception class will be the ones implementing this approach but they will need the understanding and support of everyone as we explain further on here.

When we refer to the 'EYFS team' we imply all the practitioners who work regularly together with the children and are responsible for the day-to-day care, learning, development, observation, planning and assessment of this 3 to 5 age range. When we refer to the 'lead person on the EYFS team' we mean the practitioner who is leading and managing all this professional work (for example, the lead teacher in a reception class, the pre-school leader in a voluntary group).

Being a Key Person:

It's personal *and* it's professional

'I remember when my children started – I could hardly drive home through my tears after I left them there!'

'I love making all the name cards and preparing photos on the coat pegs – it's so exciting anticipating the arrival of the new little ones.'

TABLE 4.1 We begin here by thinking about both 'personal' and 'professional' perspectives on the Key Persons approach.

It's personal	It's professional
Practitioners' attachments at home Being a Key Person in a 'family'	Practitioners' attachments at work Being a Key Person in EYFS school classes and settings
Close bonds established between practitioners' 'special' people on whom they depend for emotional support (may be partners, children, parents, or a special friend)	Being available to work to develop a close relationship with a small group of children *and* their families to whom support is offered

Elinor Goldschmied used to talk of our *'internal textbooks'*, that is, our own or personal experience of attachments from our own childhoods as well as professional experiences. The relationships with children we have loved in our own families as well as in our own classrooms and groups are important internal texts or reference points. She would emphasise the relevance of taking account of our own evidence that comes from the heart as well as the mind. We may draw on the encounters and wisdom from a close bond with teachers, colleagues and mentors who have made an impact on our approach to our work to help us to think about the significance of a child's words, actions and deeds.

Then there is the more formal evidence from research on attachment and human development (Geddes, 2006; Goldschmied and Jackson, 2004) that also help us to reflect and talk together about our observations of and relationships with the children and families in our care.

We are influenced by discussions in the literature of *'the personal in the professional'* (Robinson, 2003; Manning-Morton, 2006) where we are encouraged as practitioners to think about what attributes contribute to positive professional working and what factors may influence negative or difficult outcomes or relationships. In the past some of us were trained to behave objectively, supposedly unaffected by our personal values, beliefs and experiences. Now we are much more mindful of how our own upbringing and values influence our analysis of observations of children as well as our Key Person relationships with a child and his family. In these professionally intimate relationships we need to take account of our 'orientation' as observers. This is an orientation that will include the personal identity of the practitioner as well as her professional preoccupations (Elfer, 2006). We share the view that our experiences professionally as well as personally are valid, rich and relevant in thinking about children, and about what kinds of childhood experiences foster healthy emotional states as well as learning. This is a well-recognised contemporary trend where researchers have formed their own research questions inspired by observations and experiences with children in their own families (for example: Roberts-Holmes, 2004; Arnold, 1999, 2003; Sheilds, 2009).

So we are as we are! We are involved grandparents as well as early years professionals. Dorothy will share some of the relationships, experiences and study that inform this part of our second edition in the hope that our readers will value her perspectives, personal and professional:

My eldest grandson became 5 in 2010 and had just completed EYFS phase. His family has enjoyed reading his Foundation Stage Profile report and reflecting on his first year in the primary school in a reception class. Many times, like many other grandparents who share in the childcare of their nearest and dearest, I have had the responsibility as well as the pleasure of regular trips to and from school. I was fortunate to have been invited in and involved as a grandparent in school life. Being a family Key Person and on the outside of school, however welcoming or involving, is a personal perspective which is very different from being on the staff and inside. Many early years practitioners are involved in close relationships with their 3-/4-/5-year-olds as well as being pedagogical leaders with the youngest children in the settings and school. An observation borne out by the tearful goodbyes at the end of term for some loving and probably very tired practitioners as they waved off their groups and classes for the last time. However, this relationship can never be the same for many of us as a parent or grandparent with the lifelong devotion of unconditional love in a family.

Professionally I had spent many years in reception classrooms as a teacher, a head teacher as well as more recently as an advisory teacher. Recently we have worked with reception class teachers and primary head teachers in different kinds of local authority to think about their work to implement a Key Persons approach in school settings. This work has included introductory training, as well as longer professional development programmes with advisory teachers and managers from a few days to ongoing action research projects spanning a number of years.

My second grandson was 3 in 2010 and entered the 3 to 5 phase of the EYFS, so he is another reason why I continue to invest personal as well as professional time and energy so as to 'get it right' for the next lot of 3 to 5s embarking on the second half of their EYFS. For many years now we have worked with practitioners thinking about a Key Persons approach for under-3s but the Key Persons approach is still relatively new in settings and school groups and classes for 3 to 5s.

In addition, I am part of a mixed race family, a family with traditions, culture and beliefs from different heritages. Working with professional colleagues as well as personal experiences in my family have convinced me that the Key Persons approach has a vital role in supporting us to offer relevant experiences for children from families similar to our own as well as for children in families different from our own. We both believe that the Key Persons approach is a vital tool in achieving racial equality for all children (Brooker, 2002; Selleck, 2006a) and important for every child in forming a positive self-image and racial identity, whether from a minority or majority ethnic group. Children may be from White families born and educated in the community for many generations, or from Black minorities settled here over two or three generations, or they may be new settlers fresh to the culture of British schools and settings, or other combinations of ethnicity and class backgrounds. Increasingly we are challenged in our families as well as in our settings and schools on how best to support children from mixed race families. New research is showing how important it is for the well-being of children of mixed race, for practitioners to be able to talk to children about their mixed heritage(s), their sense of racial identity from a White as well as a Black family. We cannot support them in talking about racism unless we are open and free to discuss differences as well as similarities (Barn forthcoming). This ability to talk openly and to be at ease with difference is an important aspect of the intimate relationships of trust and mutual respect that may be built up between a child, the child's family and their Key Person at pre-school and school. This part of the Key Persons role and relationships is one that needs to be explored further if we are to be truly inclusive of children and families from diverse racial, cultural and social backgrounds.

We have experiences of implementing a Key Persons approach in different contexts and from a range of starting points that we can share. We think that there is no one way to implement this approach and what follows cannot be a manual of 'how to do it'! We hope to inspire you to have the confidence to move to the next stage of your Key Persons journey by drawing on some of our personal and professional experiences. Every practitioner has the powers of their imaginative minds and may be able to open their hearts to find their own unique way to nurture Key Person relationships in their groups.

These professional as well as personal experiences are part of our reference resources as we think about the Key Persons approach for the 3- to 5-year-olds in EYFS settings and schools.

Why do we need a Key Persons approach with 3- to 5-year-olds as well as with babies and under-3s?

'They are really quite independent by 3 – do we really need this Key Person thing? How can I explain it to the parents when they want their children to start being grown up and stop being babies?'

It may be tempting to support the views behind the question above. But judging by Helena's story (below), it is hard to doubt that 3- and 4-year-olds also need the security of a close relationship with their Key Person. Indeed, throughout our lives, especially when embarking on new ventures, we all need the security of knowing we have the attention and support of those to whom we are closest and trust the most:

> Helena's sister Alice was six months old when Helena (aged three and a half) began attending full time at the nursery. Helena was therefore well aware that her baby sister was at home occupying the nest. She was looked after alternately by her granny and her father, while Helena herself was away from home. This major encroachment by Alice on Helena's family relationships was one of the principal themes of the observation. Helena had the experience of being the only child in the family until relatively recently. She now faced in the nursery a big empty space around her, which she describes in a series of drawings done during the first observation:
>
> > Inside each border on every picture, Helena drew a zigzag line over a short distance and then drew a big H with a considerable flourishand said 'H for Helena' to herself. I noticed that Helena made a few faint half-hearted marks on the paper under the zigzag.
>
> The key issue for Helena appeared to be how to exist in this vast space? Could you still be in the picture at home? Above all, should she aim to be a big strong flourishing Helena or could there by room for a weaker, not so self assured little girl?
>
> (Dennis, 2001)

We do not know how Helena's experience at nursery developed. However, it is easy to see how much this experience might be shaped by the presence of a Key Person who would have the responsibility and time to get to know Helena and her family situation well. With this knowledge, the Key Person could then make a big difference to helping Helena feel special at nursery and able to enjoy and benefit from all that the nursery had to offer. If there had been no Key Person and if no one really had the time to think about Helena's perspective and experience, Helena might have become 'cut off' and 'quiet'. Then she may have been seen by the adults in the setting as 'having settled reasonably well', indicated by her composed behavior as she struggled to cope with her feelings alone.

There is a growing body of professional experiences which we review in the next few pages to support the Key Persons approach in EYFS settings and classes for 3- to 5-year-olds. There are three main overlapping spheres that we believe are most persuasive in emphasising why this approach needs to extend to the older children and their families – well-being, learning and development, and equality. We take each sphere in turn and indicate some of the arguments we have to show why pre-school leaders and teachers need to take this on.

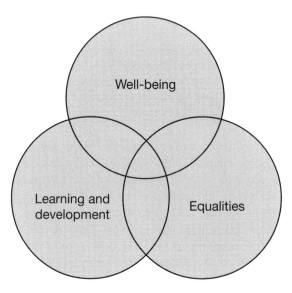

FIGURE 4.1 The three overlapping spheres that indicate the Key Persons approach should be extended to a wider age group.

Well-being

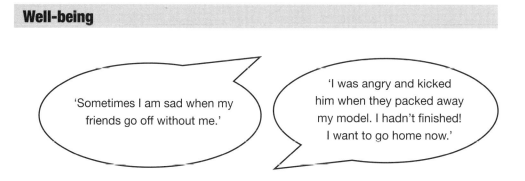

There is evidence to show that secure attachments and loving interactions between key carers in the home as well as in the settings and school are important for mental health in childhood as well as in the future. Children who do not have accessible and reliable attachment relationships with someone who is special to them and who will keep them in mind have less ability to cope with stress. Patterns of bio-chemical responses to stress may be set in childhood and leave a child later in life with a suscep-tibility to depression or aggression. One of the many places where this research is summarised is in a chapter called 'corrosive cortisol' in Sue Gerhardt's book, *Why Love Matters* (Gerhardt, 2004). Gerhardt explains that the effects of too much cortisol, an enzyme that we produce at times of fright or flight (stress) can impact on the physio-logical development of the brain. In particular it impacts on the hippocampus, which is central to learning and to memory. Gerhardt summarises the strong evidence that early care actually shapes the developing nervous system and determines how stress is interpreted and responded to in the future. Stress is part of the ups and downs of life and a healthy response to times when children are overwhelmed or feel misunderstood or excluded. This is all part of learning to belong and participate in the social groups of classrooms and outdoor learning challenges. However, prolonged, unpredictable and uncontrollable stress can be detrimental to a child's mental health in early childhood and may continue to impact on their abilities to form relationships throughout life.

So what does that mean for 3- to 5-year-olds? We know that an instigator of stress and high cortisol levels in young children is insecure attachment. That is, a lack of confidence in the child's Key Person to be emotionally available and to support them at times of frustration, challenge, rage, exuberance or desolation.

Many studies have focused on babies and under-3s and show that the main source of anxiety for the youngest children is being separated from their primary family Key Person. However, for children over age 3 increasingly their stress is about managing in groups, making friends and learning the skills and connecting cues of their peer group.

This is what some 5-year-old children said about starting school in a study focused on listening to children in Oxfordshire:

'Don't be scared, teachers are nice people.'
'Sometimes my friends go off without me.'
'I like the art bay because you get to choose who to sit next to.'

Relationships with other children were what children liked most and least about school ... A few children mentioned missing mummy and daddy ... many of their drawings depicted them playing with their friends.

(Slatter, 2005)

We know that children are dependent on adults who are tuned into their needs to help them manage; they need someone who is consistently available, who notices their feelings, who will comfort and contain their powerful emotions and support them in regulating their mighty miseries or over-the-top excitements. In practice that may mean the challenges of winning or losing, of leading the game or relinquishing the toy when it is someone else's turn.

Case study: Playing snap – winning, losing and listening (Grandma's observation diary, February 2008)

When Dorothy's grandson was 3 years old his mother brought him some 'snap', 'happy families' and 'picture lotto' cards for a long train journey.

They played them together at the kitchen table. Joshua was very able at matching the cards but found the concept of winning and losing full of anxiety. Dorothy (Grandma) 'let him win' a number of rounds of snap, (her reactions were still swifter), she beat him to the call of snap and won a round of cards yelling '*I won*' in happy celebration.

Joshua found this very distressing. First he put his head in his hands and wailed 'That's not fair.' Grandma remonstrated with him and tried to explain that sometimes she would win and at other times he would win. When the child won Grandma would say, 'Well done Joshua – that was fun' and when Grandma won he should say, 'Well done Grandma'. This led him to vehement protest and incredulous rage as he expressed his sense of betrayal and dismay that Grandma should make him suffer so when in the past their encounters had been (fairly) reliably pleasurable (e.g. completing a new jigsaw together, eating the cake they had baked, collecting treasures on their walks). Head in hands he remonstrated, 'No Grandma – that's *not fair* – my Daddy will come and chop off your head!' His mother, watching from close by, rose to protect her child when she saw how unmanageable Grandma's

FIGURE 4.2 Playing games with his father, learning to win and lose.

suggestion was for Joshua. She protested at Grandma's explanation of the 'rules' of snap. As his mother she intervened, emphasising that he had only just learnt the game, and that at 3 we should continue to enjoy the game with him on his own terms without distressing him by introducing winning and losing, which seemed to be unmanageable for him. We reflected on this. Maybe she was right. Grandma's first reaction was to be worried that he would not be able to 'play nicely' in a group with other children and instinctively she wanted to curb his shocking expostulation about cutting off her head! However, perhaps if she had been really listening to him maybe she should have understood that it is too soon and that the concepts of fairness and winning and losing may need to be for later. Grandma waited to see if on their next games encounter she had put him off playing those games altogether, or if Joshua would be able to play with her again and manage to lose gracefully? Indeed, by her next visit he had had lots of practice playing games like this with his dad. In just a week he was very able to say, 'Well done Grandma' when it was Grandma's luck to win a round, with resignation if not pleasure!

We recount this family incident by way of sharing the overwhelming power of children's emotions when they feel out of control, even when they have the language and dramatic imagination of this 3-year-old to express their outraged indignation. It also demonstrates how hard we need to work to 'get it right' by really listening to children's emotional expression and acknowledge their stress. In this case mum, dad and grandma, all key home people, worked with all their powers of love, protection, teaching and training to support the child to regulate his emotions.

By really listening to a child's voice we can resist our learnt and sometimes rigid responses set from less empathic early childhood textbooks, those in our head and heart, perhaps passed on from our own authoritarian childhoods or from guidance we have read where management of groups of children is prioritised over well-being and emotional responsiveness to each child. In the past we may have seen such expressions of rage from a child as rudeness or as a 'problem behaviour' to be 'managed' rather than working to understand it and respond to it as an expression of the child's inner world (Robinson, 2011).

In this episode Joshua's mother instinctively knew when to intervene, sensing when his fright and frustration were just too much. She was able to draw on her intimate attachment with him to curb grandma's untimely expectation of him to play by the rules. This is an example of how loving intimacy or attachment helped the child to play the game and learn the rules at his pace, rather than rejecting the games due to too much expectation of him too soon.

So what happens in settings, school groups and classrooms when children do not have their primary attachment figures from home to contain their emotions and console them? (Even more urgently, how do children who have not experienced secure primary attachments manage in settings and school? See p. 100 for a fuller discussion on this point.)

In studies of 3- and 4-year-old children in full day care settings who were separated from their primary attachment figures all day the children had high cortisol levels that increased as the day went on, even when they did not appear to be stressed (Dettling *et al.*, 1999). In a second study Dettling *et al.* (2000) found that children placed with early years professionals who were highly responsive to them had normal cortisol levels. This research seems to suggest that children can manage well with a secondary attachment figure, a Key Person, so long as she is tuned in and emotionally available to the child. On the other hand, the Dettling studies do suggest that it is the lack of this consistent responsiveness and protection that is stressful and perhaps harmful for young children.

Other studies of well-being suggest that children need companions in a shared discovery of new ways of behaving, an adult playmate who knows and likes them and who comes alongside them in their interests.

Trevarthen (1994) shows that infants even in the first year seek companionship with familiar people. The babies thrive best in a relationship that involves reciprocal transmissions of intentions, interests and feelings. He cites games of showing off, joking, and performing joint tasks as significant with special adults (parents) who know them well being crucial for the babies' well-being. Trevarthen's research strongly demonstrates how familiar adults with an ongoing involvement with children are important for children's development of self-esteem. Children who feel understood express 'being chuffed' or pleased with themselves. Children who are responded to by an adult who does not 'get it' or fails to understand the child's cues and gestures may feel disappointed or even humiliated and shamed. We would argue that in classes/groups of 3- to 5-year-olds this kind of important 'companionship' relationship with an adult is necessary for well-being and mental health. Our observations suggests that regular opportunities to experience a sense of 'companionship' do not happen reliably without a Key Person's approach where a designated member of staff can keep a few children especially in mind rather than keep an eye out for all of them. This does not mean that there is an expectation that practitioners need to be alongside their key children all the time; on the contrary, children who are securely attached to their Key Person will often be off and away with other adults and groups. It is because the Key Person has a relationship of professional intimacy that they will 'look out for' the children in their group so as to be an advocate for them with all the other staff they are playing and learning with.

In the following observation of Adam in a reception class we see how a child who reaches out to get his needs met with all his powerful strategies of playful humour, persistent good nature and creative intelligence is thwarted, frustrated and excluded without the experience of an adult who, because of the attachment bond, is able to keep him in mind, who is making it her business to be his companion in addition to her pedagogical role of someone who plans to scaffold and support his play. This observation demonstrates that Adam needs someone special, not anyone, who can help him manage the stress of joining a group and contain the desolation of being left out.

Case study: Adam – learning to be in a class group, needing a Key Person?

Context

Adam, age 5, has recently joined a reception class. His family are new to the community. Most of the other children in the class were all together in the nursery class at the same school before moving on to the reception class. The classroom environment has been developed by the children and the staff as a result of their interest in the story/video of the Titanic. In this class the children have a *real* choice in planning the curriculum. They are consulted about what they would like to learn about next and their views and ideas are listened to, noted and taken account of. The staff planned the learning environment and their teaching based on the children's interests and preoccupations.

At the time, many of the children had been watching the video at home and were preoccupied with the drama and the life under the sea. The staff had set up an imaginative and 'open ended' role play area to support the children's play and learning.

Observation (an extract from a full morning in the classroom)

At the end of a group session sitting on the floor Adam was listening as his teacher invited the children to plan their morning. She said, 'You can choose your own learning for the first part of the morning. Where are you going to start your learning?' Adam spends a brief time playing outside, then watches some girls drawing mermaids in the art/workshop area and finally settles to play in the underwater role play area. The teacher acknowledges his choice and helps him think about how to get started, 'Think who you are and how you behave', she suggests.

He peeps down the tunnel where a group of girls are looking at books – I can hear them sounding out the words. Adam calls to them "Let's play swimming first?" They do not respond and continue with their reading.

Adam jumps into the ball pool, wallows and calls to anyone who is listening, 'I am a sting ray! I am a star fish. I am happy!'

He then finds a plastic shark and makes him 'swim' in and out of the bubbles from the bubble machine. He swirls round and round dancing in the bubbles to the rhythm of the music on the tape. He catches the bubbles in time to the music. He finds another cloth shark and gestures fierce noises to the girls in the cave. There is no response.

He returns to swimming his shark through the bubbles. Adam then joins another child at the picture board of Titanic images. They talk together about the ship at the bottom of the sea in the picture.

All the other children in the group are now inside the caves. Adam begins to enter in the tunnel. The other children tell him he is going the wrong way.

He detaches the tunnel from the tent (centre of the cave) and speaks to the girl who is leading the play there, 'You are not being nice to me Ellie – I won't let you come to my birthday party.'

Adam retreats and returns to the bubbles to think about what to do next. He jumps into the ball pool, scatters the balls and laughs loudly.

He finds the octopus made of stuffed tights and throws it high in the air and watches with satisfaction as it splashes back into the ball pool.

'Ellie look at me,' he shouts. Ellie seems not to notice.

Adam then goes to a display on the window and rubs his fingers in the blue paint. He makes his blue fingers into a claw shape and has another attempt to impress Ellie and enter in the play in the caves.

He chases down the tunnel to the group of children and captures some of the wooden painted fishes in the cave, scooping them up with his 'blue claws'. 'You must share,' he entreaties as they scoop all the fishes back and pile them in the centre of their enclosure.

All the other children are now inside the tunnels and caves. 'I want to play Titanic,' he says, but no-one hears him.

'I am going to write a picture,' he tells his teacher. She helps him find some pencil and paper. He brings them to the table by me outside the underwater scene looking in. He draws the outline of a fish, colours in the eye and then gives it a face. He holds it up and calls, 'Look Ellie I did a fish!' (She is not impressed.)

He adds detail of a dorsal fin and draws bubbles rising from the fish's mouth. He starts to write and sounds out the letters to himself (see Figure 4.3). Adam turns to me and says, 'It says, "it is swimming".' He then counts the bubbles one to eight (correctly). He finds the tape dispenser and takes some sticky tape, puts a piece in each corner, takes it to the display and fixes it to the wall. He adjusts the angle and presses down the tapes to ensure it is fixed. No one seems to notice.

FIGURE 4.3 Adam's drawing of a fish.

He then returns to the ball pool and sits in one half of the scallop of balls. Ellie says, 'Boys can't go here', but then concedes, 'This one is for boys and this one is for girls.' This 'rule' effectively excludes Adam from the other scallop of balls. He says, 'No, it isn't.' 'This is girls, Adam,' Ellie insists. Adam shakes his head and says, 'No! All the balls have to stay' (in his half of the scallop shell). The girls are removing all the balls from his half of the pool.

Adam gets cross. He asserts, 'All the balls have to stay in here.' He stays calm even though the group of girls are continuing to take all the balls away from his pool.

Adam tries a different tactic. He joins in with the girls and throws more of 'his' balls into their pool. The girls take over all the balls in their half of the scallop pool.

After a bit he seems defeated and resigned. 'I don't want to play in there any more,' he says, climbs into the tunnel and looks at the four wooden fish the girls had been playing with earlier. He gathers up the wooden fish and offers them to the other children to play with in the pool. They take them but Adam is still not 'allowed' in to join the play.

He stands back and looks on as the children develop a game of eating in the ball pool. He is inspired! He says, 'I know, the orange balls can be the oranges and these (red balls) can be the strawberries. We have to have a picnic! I will get them in there for you Ellie?' The others ignore his bid to belong to the group.

Adam returns to the writing table and finds some post it notes. He writes (see Figure 4.4).

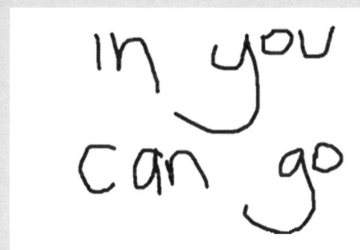

FIGURE 4.4 Adam's writing.

Adam firmly fixes his new rule to the entrance of the caves.

Unfortunately the children are now asked to regroup and tidy up. I wonder if this last strategy to be included, to make friends, to be a part of the play will succeed tomorrow?

Discussion

Adam thought of 21 different ways to 'join in'.

- How do you think he was feeling at tidy-up time?
- What types of strategies did he invent for being included?
- Do you think it may have been a different experience for Adam if he had had a Key Person and been in a key group? (He already had talented, energetic and kind teachers.)
- In what ways do you think this episode may have affected Adam's well-being?
- If you were Adam's Key Person and he had joined your group of 10 children:
    - What would you do?
    - What would you say?
    - Why do you think Adam was being excluded?
    - How might you comfort Adam and support him to fit into his new class?
    - What would you have said to the other children so that he could be accepted into the group?
    - Would you have intervened earlier? Why? How?
    - What might you want to have a conversation about with his parents?
    - How would you prepare the children in your key group for the new boy joining them to be included?

> Inclusion is a process of identifying, understanding and breaking down barriers to participation and belonging.
>
> (Early Childhood Forum, 2003)

The research questions: 'What situations and experiences support well-being and what makes a difference to practitioners' well-being?' were part of an action research project with managers and practitioners in Oxfordshire (Roberts, 2005). The findings revealed two important aspects of the Key Persons role in 3 to 5 groups. First that companionable attention that is warm, attentive and respectful enhances well-being and second that for children 'apprenticeship matters'. Roberts describes this as 'diagogy' (distinctive from pedagaogy) because it is about a child and an adult doing things together (gardening, repairing materials, preparing food, gathering logs for a building project, etc.). These kinds of 'apprenticeship' activities when the character of this relationship is that of an adult with an established and ongoing relationship with the child may be undervalued in EYFS groups and classes and are often carried out by adult helpers away from the children rather than with them. These activities could

FIGURE 4.5 Working alongside adults, building blocks for 'professional intimacy'.

be one of the building blocks for 'professional intimacy', a building of trust and an attachment relationship between a child and his Key Person or with his key group. Such attention in joint endeavours for the benefit of the group can engender feelings of well-being, inclusion and a sense of belonging. This attention has a vital role to play in enhancing children's sense of worth and confidence in their efficacy and place in the group as they contribute to the communities of their groups or classrooms. They may feel valued and useful at home but also in their school/setting communities. This is an aspect of the Key Persons approach that is important for each child's well-being.

The Key Persons approach is about a relationship with the child's parents as well as a child and there is evidence (Shields, 2009) that many parents feel less connected with reception classes than they did with their pre-school settings. This is a further reason for developing this approach in schools for the well-being of parents as well as for the children.

A focus on the final year of the EYFS: extending a Key Persons approach into primary schools and reception classes

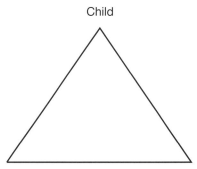

Child

Family
Key people at home
Primary family attachments

Teacher or teaching assistant
Key Person in school
A secondary attachment

FIGURE 4.6 A relationship with a family and their child: a triangle of trust and attachments in the classroom.

Many schools already go to elaborate and careful lengths to ease the transition from nursery to reception class. Plans are made in several ways for making those first days of settling in as smooth as possible. When talking to teachers and head teachers in many areas we have heard about imaginative and thoughtful strategies to welcome children into the school, including: taster visits in the summer term, home visits before starting school, open days for parents of new pupils, staggered entry, matching attendance days and times to pre-school experiences to begin with, increasing half days to full days as children and parents want it, new entrants paired with older children in buddy schemes, and so on. We have no doubt that these measures help many children and their families to feel at ease with new people, places and routines. However, in spite of these efforts our personal and professional experience is that the first few days of school are still an emotional roller coaster for many children and their parents (Selleck, 2009; Shields, 2009).

> I well remember taking one grandchild to school in his first few weeks in the reception class. It was a challenging time for our family where both parents and grandparents work. We each took a week off so as to take and collect him for the half day place he was allocated for the first half term. This was a difficult transition for us as he had been used to full day care and could not make sense of why he had to go home and miss lunch and the afternoon when he was used to a full day and being picked up in time to go home for tea. In addition we had been accustomed to a gentle start at handover times in the morning and time for a chat with his Key Person at the reunion at the end of the day. This is usual good practice in most nurseries. In contrast the first mornings at the primary school felt abrupt and impersonal. Parents and children gathered in the playground apprehensive and excited, with their young children looking proud and small inside their new uniforms. When the classroom doors opened the children all disappeared inside past an imperceptible barrier of the teacher and her assistant. There was no handover ritual, no personal welcomes and no personal goodbye for grandma either! On that first morning I felt left on the outside, uncertain that he was gone or was at ease inside. Even though he had rushed into the classroom his arm entwined round his new friend and was eager to begin his day I was uncomfortable, even disconsolate. Would he come out again in a minute to wish me goodbye, would he think I had abandoned him if I left? Should I stay? Should I go? Other parents drifted away and after peering in at the window to reassure myself that he was in the flow of new friends I left too. As I walked down the path I felt I had failed him, I felt I had not said goodbye 'properly' or ensured that the teachers had noticed he was there. After that we created our own goodbye ritual of handing over water bottles and book bags with hugs for me and his younger brother. This created a definite parting, and a certain start to a school day for both of us. Indeed by the end of the week I found a pretext for going into the classroom for him to show me something he wanted me to share. When I asked the staff if I could go in they were very welcoming. I enjoyed chatting with his teacher and we had a few unhurried minutes so that he could show me his classroom and all the wonders of play and adventure that were impressive and important to him. It was obvious that the staff had made playful and thoughtful preparations in the learning environment to make it inviting for their new little ones. However, it was telling that when I rejoined the other parents and grandparents outside in the playground where we gathered to get to know each other at the end of each day, that one mother exclaimed enviously, 'How on earth did you manage to get in? I would love to see inside!'

At the other end of the year I appreciated all the efforts the staff made to emphasise a warm and friendly family atmosphere in the school and I think they would be shocked to know how awkward and difficult the first few weeks were for some parents.

(A personal experience – Dorothy)

This bears out for us how partnership with parents cannot be personal and effective if we hand our children over to 'all of them' or even 'both of them' (teacher and teaching assistant) rather than to someone, a Key Person who we know is going to take a special interest in our child. Welcome packs and parents' evenings cannot take the place of a personal relationship of trust between a particular member of staff with a child and a family.

This personal experience is echoed in a research study of parents' negative experiences of their children starting school. One parent described his literal exclusion from the school's systems:

we hung around outside, milling about, and then the teachers would show up just before nine, and then they would open the doors for the kids but the kids weren't allowed in … (later) they tell me … the classroom stays locked till nine, … reception kids have to wait outside in a line. So I thought, OK, I did two open days, an induction night, and I had an information pack, and I didn't know any of that stuff! And I thought that's practical stuff I would liked to have known.

(Shields, 2009: 244)

Shields says that the parents' testimonies in her study demonstrate that a closer partnership is both needed and desired by parents. Parents reported that they felt it was up to them to approach the school when they felt excluded, that they would have to make the effort to communicate. Parents felt the emphasis had changed to education and learning and were worried that there was less concern than in the nursery for the well-being of their child. The parents perceived that there was emphasis on the curriculum rather than their child as a person. A line had been drawn between home and school culture which they interpreted as a sign that their input was no longer welcome or necessary.

This small study chimes with the findings and recommendations of the much more extensive Cambridge Primary Review (Alexander *et al.*, 2009). The final report appeals to early years teams:

good relations between early years settings and primary schools are essential … fundamental is the need for better home school communications, crucially going out and talking to parents rather than waiting for them to ask for help.

As professionals on the inside we know it is not the intention or perception of most reception class teachers that they are not connecting enough with parents. Indeed reception class staff do devote much energy to ensuring the new pupils in the school settle in and that parents are initiated into the culture of the school. However, if we listen to such studies, reports and personal stories as have been described here, then there is a compelling rationale for introducing a Key Persons approach to reception classes for the final year of the EYFS for the well-being of both parents and children. If parents know that someone in particular rather than everyone, anyone or no one on the staff is keeping them and their child in mind with regular personal and informal contacts perhaps we can improve.

Many Key Persons in schools that are developing this approach are finding ways of communicating and building the relationship with their small group in the way that suits both parties best. For many it will be the day-to-day personal contacts at the beginning or end of the school day but for working parents new technologies as well as the traditional methods of communication have provided contemporary possibilities for reciprocal interchanges. Text messages, email, phone, faxes, and Skype are all ways in which some Key People make exchanges with some parents of children in their group. In addition the more traditional options such as: home visits before starting and half way through the school year; outreach days; home school diaries; parents' social networks to support key groups all play a part in establishing and nurturing the Key Person relationship. This is a relationship that is personal to a child and his or her parents. It is important to emphasise that different families and different Key People can select the ways to keep in touch that suit each pair best.

In addition to these personal conversational Key Person exchanges there are other strategies to keep parents informed. The duplicated newsletters, reminders, 'dates to note' charts, suggestions for practising at home with spellings, high-frequency words to learn so as to support literacy, or suggested activities for 'homework' to follow up school interests are all examples of what some schools tuck into the book bags to carry home or post on the school website. These are more whole class/school ways of offering information to parents. These messages to parents are so that they can know what is on offer and what is expected of them to support their child's learning and for them to be able to take part in the school community. They are school initiatives to build a partnership with parents that are universal to all the children's parents.

A distinction needs to be made between the whole school strategies for keeping all parents informed and the more intimate and personally crafted ideas for being in a relationship with a child's Key Person. The Key Person relationship is an evolving affiliation in bringing up a child as co-carers and educators with respect for and account taken of the professional contribution as well as the family perspective. This kind of personalised reciprocity can only happen with a small group of children. For example, it would be unrealistic to expect a lead teacher to email every child's family in the class regularly! But it is feasible for a Key Person to do that for the two or three children in her group whose parents need or want that. Some parents may prefer this more private way of exchanging rather than the public spaces of the classroom or playground at the end of the day. Other parents without access to the Internet or who prefer face-to-face contact will not want to choose this way to connect with their Key Person. A few children in the key group may need support with translators or go-betweens who speak a home language. Again this is more manageable if a Key Person is able to build a relationship with a few rather than for all the children and families for whom English is a second language. There will need to be a translator that the family and the Key Person are able to trust to understand and communicate messages accurately and in confidence.

There are many ways in which some schools work to establish the triangle of trust between a unique child and his family. However, in the end a meaningful, trusting three-way relationship can only be built little by little. What matters overall is the time, energy, commitment and support to build a partnership that can bear it when there are difficult things to be discussed. Practitioners may sometimes feel frustrated or angry when they think a parent's behaviour is not helping a child to settle. Parents may be angry or hurt when they feel 'talked down to' by a teacher, or not honestly talked to at all.

Our experience of talking with early years teachers raises a number of barriers to building this triangle of trust encapsulated in the speech bubbles below. Look to the end of this chapter for fuller practical guidelines for starting to implement a Key Persons approach in terms of allocating children and setting up Key Person groups in the primary school (see pp. 112–17). There are also case studies in the final chapter of this book where primary school staff describe how they found successful ways of implementing this way of working over time. However, here we explore some of these issues that may get in the way of getting started or that seem insurmountable or unnecessary about the Key Persons approach in school.

'We can't possibly have an attachment with 26 plus children and their families. Even if we could divide them 10/15 each the teacher is, in the end, responsible for all of them.'

'We know all the children really well anyway, so there is no need for all this Key Persons stuff – we do it already.'

It is understandable that teachers are mindful of taking on the possible and manageable rather than getting drawn into a way of working that would seem to be overcomplicated or could undermine their familiar tried and tested ways of managing their responsibility for planning and assessing each child's learning, progress and attainment. It is of course impossible to have the kind of relationship described above with all the children in the class and in the Key Persons approach the children will be in smaller groups with other members of the EYFS team. For teachers this will mean handing over the relationship with a child and a family, in groups other than her own, to the teaching assistants (TAs). The part of the relationship that is to do with emotional support, and more intimate involvement with the family will be entrusted to someone else. The teacher continues of course to have overall responsibility for planning and learning however much the other members of the team are able to, or choose to, or are delegated to take on the work of observation, planning, documentation and assessment. The issue here for foundation stage teachers is about leading a team, and the implications of sharing the children. This means relinquishing overall control, learning to trust, train and allow other partners in the team to build close relationships with a few of the children in the class. This has long been established practice in nurseries where teachers and nursery nurses have worked as partners with shared responsibilities and pooled expertise and experience. There are many practical barriers that are raised by some teachers who think that the TAs are not qualified enough or 'up to the job'. Even so, in our experience (exemplified by the case studies at the end of the book from Manchester and Oxfordshire) Key Person relationships are about people-to-people work and do not depend on qualifications. Building trust, tuning into another's anxiety or preoccupations requires empathy, attention, listening skills, kindness, and a lively interest in people like ourselves as well as different from ourselves. These are all qualities that can be developed by all of us over time with support, supervision and time to talk together as a team to share the challenge. Most people who take up work in schools, both teachers and TAs, are there because they enjoy the involvements they have with children and their families and in our experience the opportunity and the responsibility of being a Key Person to a few children in the class is very rewarding and enjoyable, most of the time. The EYFS team are still a team and when a child or the family need special attention, when they are in trouble, have problems or are anxious then the concerns – within confidential boundaries – can be shared and thought about together. The EYFS team led by the teacher can think together about the best way to respond to a child or their family. Support from each other or other professionals may be sought where that is helpful. Then it is the role of the Key Person assigned to the child and the family to do the talking, offer the solace, suggest a plan, or help with practical details as they are the ones who are building that special bond with the child and his family. This part of the job is experienced by many Key Persons as well worth the personal and professional commitment of the time and energy that it requires. This professional relationship can be a reciprocal triad of interchanges and shared encounters that make up the triangle of trust and shared work of ensuring a child is safe and secure as they begin their school life.

Knowing all the children in the class well and being in an affectionate, friendly relationship with them all is important for every teacher but that relationship is different from the more intimate involvements of the Key Person bond. We have struggled to describe this here and the following story in the box below helped us to think about it together. Maybe this story will have resonances for you too? The accounts from other practitioners in the final chapter will also illustrate the distinctive and more intimate nature of the Key Person's involvement with a child and a family.

Memories of being a class teacher in a reception class (from Dorothy)

I worked hard with my first reception class of 45 children with the help of a wonderful nursery nurse who helped me in the morning as much as her other responsibilities in the school allowed. Forty-plus years later I still remember many of the children's names and in a drawer in the spare room I still cherish some of the letters and drawings that they gave me at the end of the year depicting shared encounters, warm wishes, sad goodbyes – not to mention copious kisses. Estelle, Richard, Suzanne, Kevin and all the others, if you read this Miss P would love to know what happened to you all! I was 22 and thought I knew and loved them all dearly. I believed that if I worked hard, prepared my lessons and resources diligently and imaginatively then I was doing a good job. In fact others thought I was doing a good job too and very soon I was promoted to a management position in the school ahead of some other more experienced teachers.

However, looking back, rather than feeling proud and pleased as I did at the time I am ashamed of many of the strategies I used to be efficient, to meet the targets we had at the time, to impress the parents and school managers who all thought I was the bees knees. All right, I was good at 'classroom management' and I glowed with the assurance and omnipotence of knowing I was doing what I was expected to do – but – years later I am not so certain, not so assured, but wiser and hopefully more able to really listen to children and parents. How did I meet that target of hearing every child read every day? I did it by juggling children – 'listening' to at least four children at once! How did I achieve all those amazing art works that 'decorated' the school corridor and impressed all the visitors? Yes, they were the work of the children but not always their creations. I sometimes thought of the ideas and the children were set to work – like a mini factory they would get sticking and pasting. I feel deeply sad that I wronged those children, that I was so bossy and did not have time or the understanding to nurture their own powers as artists.

I could choose to tell you the stories I am still proud of, there were children in that group of 45 with whom I did make an attachment and I did nurture some of their talents – but too often with too many I didn't … I may have had the respect of colleagues and parents but not the families' confidences or the maturity or awareness of each child's emotional needs and unique contributions.

Over the years I have learnt to relinquish my powers to manage and control and have become more open to uncertainty, and to ponder on possibilities that emerge from really listening. I work hard not to see children's needs or interests in my own terms of what they must learn or achieve but by standing in a child's shoes and observing we now all try to work harder to build on what children know, can do and understand. We work to empathise with their feelings and ideas rather than impose our own (limited) notions of what is planned or possible. In this way children and families have a way 'to be', to contribute and participate in a more equitable and shared partnership.

As I support and mentor practitioners today I know that the Key Persons approach makes this way of working more likely to be a reality rather than a vain aspiration or a mistaken assumption.

It really isn't possible to know all of them well enough, to build relationships with the parents of children who are not always forthcoming or are diffident, who may be speaking English as an additional language, who may be unfamiliar with how schools operate, for parents with children who have special or additional needs, or to get to know families like ours as well as like yours unless we have a Key Persons approach. Even in a class of 30 with three full-time early years practitioners in the team each of us can only keep a small group of children in mind. We may have that sixth sense alert which 'looks out' for children in need of containment or help with regulating their emotions. Only with a small number of children can we have that invisible elastic connection with a particular child which means that a glance, a word, a gentle touch, or holding at the right moment will buoy them on to manage in a big group, will keep them secure and sustain their access to all the experiences available in the school environment.

Learning and development

> 'So the Key Persons approach is more than just "settling" children? Could it make a difference to our assessments of their progress and achievements?'

In this section we will demonstrate how important a Key Persons approach is for children's cognitive development and their learning in pre-school settings and school classrooms.

The Effective Provision of Pre-School Education (EPPE) study (DfES, 2004) and Millennium Cohort Study (MCS) (Mathers *et al.*, 2007) report a wide range of detailed findings on early years provision, mainly consistent with each other and with earlier research reviews (Melhuish, 2004). The MCS data, coming five years on from the EPPE data, showed significant improvements in setting standards, particular in the quality of language, reasoning and general interactions between staff and children. However, on 'diversity' ('diversity' here refers to staff responses to children as individuals, e.g. planning activities suited to children of different abilities and responsive to racial and cultural diversity) scores remained unchanged. They were poor in the EPPE results and remained so in the MCS results. Unfortunately, the MCS data did not take account of Key Person practices in early years settings so it is not possible to say whether or how Key Persons approaches may or may not have been associated with levels of attention to individual children. However, it would seem very likely that the more widespread practice of the Key Persons approach would improve levels of individual attention as described above.

A child's access to learning opportunities is dependent on healthy emotional states. If a child's resources are focused on managing stress then they will not have access to the learning experiences planned for them. Energy and curiosity are reduced if children are seeking unavailable secure bases, or attachment figures to validate or share in their concerns and interests. So it is important that all the EYFS team working in settings and schools, including teachers and their assistants in EYFS classrooms, are cognisant of the emotional and attachment needs of children in their care (Robinson, 2011; Geddes, 2006; Read, 2010). When a child enters their new group or class, whether it is the bustling, blooming confusion of a garden play area, or having to offer his own ideas or story in a bumptious, competitive 'carpet time' gathering, or managing new stiff uniforms after a summer of shorts and T shirts, these may all be moments when a child can feel small and overwhelmed by the demands of 'BiG' school or of attending the pre-school for the first time. These are instances when a child may be unable to focus or hear what is said to them, times when they are in the individual moment of their unique experiences of tension or dismay. It is in these moments when he relies on an adult with whom he feels a special connection to be there, to come alongside his fearfulness, contain his trepidation and enable him to feel understood and supported so as to re-enter and regain his sense of being included in the excitement of new tasks and challenges. Practitioners work hard to create these new learning tasks and challenges, making them playful and developmentally appropriate. However, unless there is someone who is in tune with each child's emotional state and interests then these curriculum plans can by-pass individual children.

This is a complex and skilful business. Planning for 30 unique children all together in a reception class or in a 60 place nursery coping with half day places morning and afternoon draws on all the training and experience of managers. We know that planning must be based on a unique child's needs and preoccupations. A Key Persons approach means children have time in cosy small groups with a predictable member of staff at the same time and place in a reassuring routine (see practical ways to be a Key Person in a reception class in Read, 2010: 74, Grenier et al., and Selleck in *The Social and Emotional Aspects of Development* (SEAD) materials, National Strategies Early Years 2008). In these small groups of children each member of the EYFS team is able to build a more professionally intimate conversation with shared social references, humour and informal physical closeness. The Key Person can then be a valuable advocate for the children in her/his group when the lead teacher/pre-school leader collates the EYFS teams' ideas for planning or assessment. Figure 4.7, of key group time in a children's centre with 3- and 4-year-olds, exemplifies this informality and intimacy. Children are sprawled and snuggling informally rather than sitting with legs crossed and ready to put their hands up in answer to a question as they might be being trained to do in the whole group. The children and practitioner are a huddle of shared interest rather than adult-led teaching sessions. The children drape and loll and lean freely in a communication of bodies as well as minds and voices. This is an intimate group of more private and personal encounters that would not necessarily be appropriate with everyone. Whole class/group times are more about learning to talk up in front of everyone, belonging and contributing to the more public forums of being in the whole group or school. These are times when everyone assembles to celebrate a festival or enjoy special news, achievements or visitors together. Key group times are a focus for shared intimacies, personal encounters and for building a trusting bond with a few other children with their shared special adult/Key Person (Selleck, 2010). A relationship with a Key Person that may over time and with the continuity of ongoing input become the 'island of intimacy' (Goldschmied and Jackson, 2004) described by the practitioners who have implemented this way of working.

FIGURE 4.7 Key group time at Eastwood Children's Centre, Roehampton. Comments from Alex Cole, the Key Person: 'Prior to these pictures being taken my key group and I had been on a Forest School session collecting objects. I had planned to use this key group time to look at our collections and talk about our experience. However, the children had different ideas. After our welcome song a child noticed a small caterpillar on another child's leg. The children were very interested. We gave him a home with a pot and leaves and watched him move.'

For some children, learning in settings and schools may be especially difficult and demanding. It can be a struggle to concentrate for children who have formed insecure attachments in their early childhood or have experienced broken ties with their Key Persons at home. This may be because of unavoidable miseries that many families have from time to time. This could be for many reasons that may include: parental illness, a mother's postnatal depression, loss of a parent, fragmented experiences of relationships experienced by children pre-adoption, serial foster carers for children being 'looked after' in local authority care, the unhappy traumas of children who have fled with their families to escape war or strife to seek refuge or asylum and find a new home far from their old ties in a new and different culture, families undergoing separation or reforming as parents settle with new partners. In other words, this can be true for many children in most EYFS groups/classes by the time they are 3 years old. So tuning into the circumstances and families of each child must be important to ensure all our children have equal chances to play and learn.

Therapists working with children with challenging behaviour sometimes identify absent or insecure primary family attachments as the basis for a child's struggles to express their feelings and to regulate their responses to others (aggressive or disruptive behaviour). Their feelings of being an outsider in learning groups (quiet withdrawal to the sidelines) may also go unnoticed. These children can miss out on learning as their stress can dislocate, literally 'locate' them away from the place they are in to a place of 'fright or flight' away from the stories, creations and discoveries going on around them. The child's lack of trust, their frightening experiences of not having had loving and consistent boundaries or of feeling valued in affectionate, responsive embraces are wobbly foundations for playing and learning. Therapists stress how important it may be for such children and for their families, who may have mental health problems, to have a special adult in settings and school (Gerhardt, 2004; Geddes, 2006). A Key Person is needed who may tune into the child's anxiety or pave the way for them to not be exposed in a way that would be difficult to cope with in settings and school.

A Key Person in the setting/school may form a close bond with the child and their home carers/family to ameliorate the effects of broken attachments so as to rebuild the trust needed for children's own confidence and for their unique powers to explore and learn to flourish. In a relationship with a Key Person children may be freed to express emotions and have them accepted.

How can the Key Persons approach work with large numbers?

Although all staff may aspire to support all children, it seems to me this is asking the impossible for one teacher/lead practitioner with 30/60 children. However sensitive and devoted to the children in her care, this is an unattainable undertaking. It is so much more likely that a child would have this kind of ally in adversity, an advocate who understands that the child's behaviour is the outward expression of their inner world (Robinson, 2011) rather than wilful mischievousness or obstreperousness if there is someone special who is keeping him in mind, rather than all of the kind adults. A Key Person who has a *small* group of children and their families with whom she has worked to form a special relationship so that she knows more about their circumstances and culture is more likely to be taken into their confidence. This kind of 'professional intimacy' (Elfer, 1996) can only happen with a few and is not possible with everyone in the class/group. You may have 30/60 'friends' on a social networking site, or on your mobile phone but the intimacies of family, fears and frights, ambitions and aspirations, trials and tribulations, losses and separations, reunions and celebrations are likely to be only shared with a few confidants.

In EYFS reception classes it is important to have full-time designated teachers and teacher's assistants so that the key groups have one adult to 10 children. This may be a deployment and funding issue for some primary schools where head teachers and governors will need to understand and support the EYFS staff team to work in this way.

Some families will need specialised help that is beyond the Key Persons role or training. It is important that EYFS teams know when and how to seek that support from co-professionals (for example, educational psychologists, therapists, social workers, etc.). Senior staff who take on the role of mentoring and supervision for the Key Person role will also need training for this aspect of their work so as to manage the boundaries of these relationships (see Aspect 4, pp. 61–7).

Where pre-schools and primary schools have embraced the Key Persons approach and have adapted their staffing and routines accordingly it is possible to implement Key Person principles and practice with 3- to 5-year-olds in large groups. At the end of this chapter we set out a number of practical suggestions for getting started on this approach and in Chapter 5 there are examples of how practitioners experienced in implementing the approach describe how it is working and developing in their setting or school.

Other research too underpins the inseparable connection between a child's emotional experiences and his/her play and learning interests. In a study of 58 children aged 2 to 4 years with their families and Key People over four years Arnold demonstrates that repeated patterns of action (schemata) are prompted by emotional needs. Her case study of Edward from when he was 2.9 to 4.3 years follows his explorations in the nursery (Arnold, 2009). Her analysis, drawn from schematic theory (Athey, 2007), as well as her study of attachment and psychoanalytical theory illuminates her detailed observations of Edward's strong interest in his play for connecting and disconnecting. (He plays with tape to mend or to connect a broken visor on a helmet. He 'fixes' the filter, hose and wheels on a vacuum cleaner and he shows persistence and satisfaction in repeating these actions.) The nursery had offered him these play materials so as to build on his cognitive interest in how machines work, of mending things, his schematic interest in disconnecting and connecting and maybe reversibility too. However, Arnold adds to this analysis in attachment terms by suggesting his play represented 'together' and 'apart' in relationships where he was thinking about his separation from attachment figures at home. These connections may represent his emotional work to reassure himself that he could come back together and be whole again with his mother.

These interpretations of behaviour may not be an approach familiar to staff trained for the 3 to 5 age group. Arnold suggests that by recognising what may be the emotional motive behind children's thinking revealed in their play behaviour we can better match our responses to their imaginings, offer materials that can extend their play and ensure a more meaningful involvement for this age group than the imposition of 'structured play' ideas created by diligent adults away from the children. Play ideas that may entertain and educate a class/group and are aimed at 'all of them' rather than 'some of them' can miss the mark. Plans that are not based on the kind of loving and reflective observations exemplified in Arnold's study that pay attention to the attachment needs of this age group may be undervaluing the child's overriding needs to self-regulate their emotions and express their stress of separation from primary attachment people at home. Children need to accommodate the ordinary to-ings and fro-ings of relationships and *feel* secure – as well as *being* safe with other trusted adults. Plans for effective practice across all four themes of the EYFS must take account of each child's emotional as well as cognitive preoccupations. Then only can we engage their attention and generate 'sustained shared thinking' (EYFS Guidance, DCSF, 2007b/2008) that is so vital for learning.

What are the implications for practice?

The importance of detailed observations

However important planning in EYFS staff teams is, however essential it is to make time for reflective discussion in staff meetings and professional development sessions, if this is not based on the loving observations made by an adult who is in a special Key Person relationship with a child and his/her family then we cannot begin to claim that we

> build conditions for learning for unique children who develop at different rates, have different interests, come from varied cultural backgrounds and unique families.
> (National Strategies, 2009)

The Key Person's role is the link that makes this and a creative, collaborative group EYFS team endeavour possible. It is a joint effort, rather than a burden to manage a big group of children by one adult in charge. This is the solution to really engaging in child-led learning and development. This is the comfort of knowing that children can stay being little children who play and use their own powers to discover and learn rather than us having to turn them into pupils before they are ready. EYFS practitioners too can have the pleasure of giving children the emotional time and space to make the transition from early childhood to being school pupils, from attachments to special adults to the companionship and camaraderie of belonging in bigger school groups, from being in relationships of healthy emotional dependence to gradually developing the emotional resilience and inner resources to go it alone while away from home.

The importance of authentic conversational exchanges between adults and children

Finding opportunities for 'sustained shared thinking' is a concept necessary for learning in young children (DCSF, 2007b/2008: 9, para 1.28) where it is defined as having these features:

- Adults are aware of the children's interests and understandings and the adults and children work together to develop an idea or skill.

- Practitioners support and challenge children's thinking by getting involved in the process with them.

- Positive trusting relationships between adults and children.

- Adults show genuine interest, offer encouragement, clarify ideas and ask open questions which supports and extends children's thinking and helps them to make connections in learning.

These are all characteristics of the Key Person's role but of course children in settings and schools will also benefit from diverse inputs from adults other than their Key Person. This includes the companionable encounters they will have with all the adults in settings and schools. These adult encounters may be with: parent helpers, lunchtime staff, students and all the visiting specialists or community people who from time to time have an involvement in their activities. These acquaintances are a rich complement to the learning environment and ensure that children have opportunities to learn from people with different skills, experiences, communities and cultures – even men, who are sadly so rarely a regular part of EYFS staff teams – but that is an issue for another place! We want our children to be outgoing and off and away with all the adults and other children much of the time by the time they are 3 years old. This is what is sometimes referred to as 'independence' in the EYFS guidance. However, this kind of 'independence' grows when securely attached children can rely on their Key Person at key times of the day. That is, there is someone with whom they can 'touch base'. It is a prerequisite for access to the wider learning environment for each child to have a dependable, secure attachment relationship so that they may then learn from and with all the other people and places in the setting and school.

What we are arguing for here is the importance of these encounters and conversations to be in addition to and to build on the foundation for learning from the Key Person role. We may all think that we are talking to the children much of the time but there is evidence that many of the interactions with children in our settings and schools are one-way rather than genuinely reciprocal. Adults are more used to asking children to recall a fact, experience, or tell them how they are expected to behave, or ask them to make a decision based on a limited selection of choices offered rather than 'sustained shared thinking'. This is not a real two-way conversation. Maybe this is less achievable in the pedagogical talk of whole group or even small group adult-led sessions. However, during a child's free play sessions there is still evidence of this lack of reciprocity in adults' support for children's play. In one study of 3 and 4 year olds 94.5 per cent of all interactions were like this (Siraj-Blatchford and Manni, 2008). Analysis showed that higher cognitive outcomes were associated with sustained adult–child verbal interactions. It stressed the importance of effective pedagogic interaction where two or more individuals 'work together' in an intellectual way to solve a problem, clarify a concept, evaluate activities or extend a narrative. This kind of 'sustained shared thinking' was subsequently found to occur most commonly in one-to-one adult child interactions.

This is more confirmation of the need for every child to have a Key Person in the nursery and in reception classes. The organisation of the Key Persons approach means it is more likely that there will be opportunities for one-to-one interactions. However, even if the opportunity is more frequent in this way of working for intimate conversational exchanges it will still depend on ensuring that all practitioners are trained and mentored to develop these kinds of open ended discussion skills, to really listen to children, to take account of their thinking, and to be able to tolerate the uncertainty of not knowing what might come next. Practitioners need to bear with the unpredictability of children's interests, and have the willingness to accept that children may initiate unanticipated enquiries even when their thread of thinking does not chime with our own enthusiasms or talents.

This concept is further underlined in a review of 500 published sources from many countries to contribute to the debate about children's well-being and education. An interim report emphasised that:

- Learning in young children is socially mediated. Families, carers and teachers are all important.
- There is a need for pretend play in the early years to enable concentration.
- In primary classrooms children seldom have the opportunity to engage in productive social interaction.

(Alexander *et al.*, pre-publication press release Dec. 2007)

The final report (Alexander *et al.*, 2009) recommends that the EYFS be extended to age 6 so that children have more time for this kind of playful and interactive learning in genuine rather than contrived conversations so that they may glide to rather than trip into the primary phase of education.

The challenge to build a strong partnership with home

The following example demonstrates how important connections between 'Key People' at home as well as in school are for children in becoming literate in expressing their ideas and making their feelings heard. Joshua, in his first term in year one, had a piece of homework which was to write his own book about the adventures of Sam and his Blanket after having had the first sample instalment read to him in his class group. This was an exciting opportunity for him but his powers of imagination were way ahead of his skills to write or read what he wanted to say so his mother had scribed his narrative and typed up another chapter each evening ready for him to take his 'book' into school (and send to grandparents by email):

Chapter 2
Sam went on holiday without his Mummy and Daddy but with Blanket and his Grandma to Egypt. Grandma said he could go and explore. Sam went to dig in the sand and he found a fossil. It was a very, very big dinosaur bone. It was heavy and Sam went to ask some people if they could help him move the fossil. They used Blanket to keep it safe so they could show Grandma. They kept Blanket safe on the

way home on the aeroplane. At home they kept it safe in the spare bedroom and then Sam took it to school to show at show and tell time.

(Joshua, age 5.9, Year 1, 2010)

With help from his Key People at home Joshua enjoyed this opportunity to be the author of his own story rather than feeling defeated by writing for homework. As he confided to grandma, 'We do a lot of writing [at school] and it is a bit new and hard for me.' He looked forward to having his 'book' read in class. We (his family) do not know what happened next but his teacher may have had an insight into how in a new class with a new teacher his narrative is expressing pleasure and confidence in his adventures but also hints at his need to be *safe*, back at home, as he identifies with the Blanket. 'Safe' is a word he used three times in this instalment of his story. On the other hand, in the midst of demands with 30 children in the class I would not be at all surprised if this important communication was overlooked and lost.

If there had been a Key Person in his school for his family to talk to the family could have shared ideas of how to support him in his frustration with writing, and been an advocate for explaining how writing was hard for him. Joshua's mother found many ways in the following weeks to support his writing at home and make the challenge less daunting and practice writing playful. Joshua enjoyed his own note-books for scribing his own sentences and seeing if we could read them back. It gave him pleasure to realise that he could indeed be creative and understood in writing. He sometimes even invited us to write something in his notebook, a message or aide memoir of how to spell words that interested him. They were kept in his pocket, or by the kitchen table and he loved 'writing' in them when waiting for meals or amusing himself after school. At this time his drawings were often enhanced with 'writing' to signify speed or sound tracks! The following drawing was just one of a whole series of fluid line drawings completed in a few minutes to express the speed and excitement of his snow sledging. 'Wheeeee!' he said as he wrote a stream of WWWWWs sliding down the hill. Another row of SSSSSs also represented the sssssspeed of the sliding and tumbling decent in the snowy field. Emergent writing shapes were spontaneous and satisfying to him and a balance to the laboured though neater and more formal adult initiated writing tasks he was coping with at school (Figure 4.8).

If only there had been a chance for his Key People at home and someone who was special for him and his family at school to talk with, then what was beginning to be an aversion to writing could have been averted jointly. His enjoyment of using words and letters to express his meanings and experiences could have been sustained alongside the challenge and motivation of the class writing lessons at school. Becoming literate and confident could have been a shared experience and aspiration for a child, his parents and teacher rather than being parallel literacy experiences in the two separate worlds of home and school.

We have talked with Foundation Stage staff who have implemented a Key Persons approach with this older age group and there is emerging evidence that scores on the Foundation Stage profile at the end of the reception year seem to be improving. As children are observed more closely, engaged in more authentic conversational exchanges with someone who knows them really well, and there are better links with

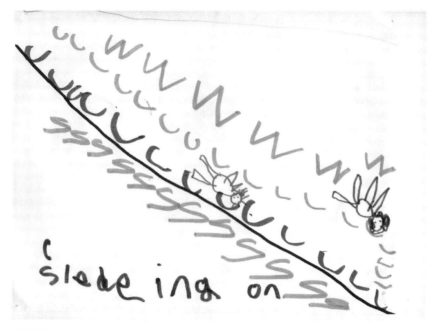

FIGURE 4.8 Joshua's drawing, age 6.2, sledging very fast.

home, it may be expected to have an impact on learning and development for each child in a class.

'I'm sure the way the staff have developed our Key Persons approach this year is the real basis of why this cohort achieved so well with EYFSP.'

Sarah Hall,
Stockham Primary School,
Oxfordshire

Suzanne Jones,
Ashbury Meadow Primary School,
Manchester

'Working in key groups has given us, the children and staff, the opportunity to work in smaller groups – developing the children's personal, social and emotional skills in this type of supportive environment, is both comforting and reassuring. Our groups provide opportunities to interact with others, to develop relationships and to become a member of a close group of friends.'

Equality

'Now Amina is going to school she wants to wear her Al-mira like her sisters. I am worried how the other children and staff will react. Who will protect her if others are mean to her?'

'Jodie's cousins have two mothers. We are in and out of each other's houses all the time. I hope when she goes to nursery they will not make her feel odd or wrong.'

The role of Key Person is important for *all* children. It is a fundamental equality issue. When a Key Person is working with a small group of children and their parents then there is much more opportunity or likelihood that he/she may form professionally intimate relationships over time that are attuned to a family's race, culture, religion, home language(s), abilities, preoccupations and special needs. We know how important the Key Person role is in working with a child and his/her family in supporting well-being, cognition, early language acquisition and literacy skills so that they may make better progress later with school language literacy and maths. This is crucial to enable children, especially those who may be disadvantaged by poverty and social circumstances, or isolated by racial prejudice and discrimination or lack of understanding, to thrive in the learning environment of school.

Many settings and some schools already work at the Key Persons approach, regardless of whether it is a formal requirement or not, as they are convinced by their own study and professional experiences of its importance. However, the EYFS has emphasised that this is so important, it is a statutory requirement, not only recommended as good practice. There has been great progress over the last 20 years to ensure each child is not cared for by multiple carers over their EYFS years so that his uniqueness may not get overlooked. It is especially important that a child who is different from the majority is not expected to assimilate to a uniform school identity that conceals his ethnic, cultural and family identity. Every child and their family needs to feel welcomed and that what they bring from their home background is relevant. Settings and schools need to be places that are enriched by diverse family contributions. Each of us in each of our families needs to feel that our choices and traditions of child rearing are recognised and that the heritage(s) we bring to the school/setting are appreciated and taken account of.

There are many documented examples where practitioners with the best of intentions have missed opportunities to welcome diversity, or have inadvertently ignored racial and cultural sensitivities, or denigrated an aspect of some belief or behaviour that seemed 'other' to them (Connolly, 1998; Brooker, 2002; Roberts-Holmes, 2004; McCreery *et al.,* 2007; Lane, 2008). These studies are not intended to 'pick on' people doing their best. Rather, we hope the following examples will be further investigated by readers who want to understand better so as to try to 'get it right' for all children in their key group in what has been described as 'a no blame culture' (Lane, 2008: 56–9).

The study of 4-year-old Jake (Roberts-Holmes, 2004) by analysing his conversations and drawings at home illustrates how intelligently and creatively Jake shapes his own racialised identity as a mixed race boy. His drawings of differences in hair types of his friends and family – 'curly and flat' – and his conversations about skin tone – 'I am a little bit brown like mummy and a little bit white like daddy' – show that his dialogue and drawings demonstrate his competency in managing the fluidity of his identity in differing situations as he describes himself as 'black brown' rather than Black or White. The discussion in this paper about a young child's racialised identity construction offers much of interest to early years practitioners. When Jake's father had attempted to share Jake's work with the practitioners at his nursery their response was dismissive, if not defensive. The possibility of further discussion was brushed aside with, 'Oh! That is no problem …'.

What did the staff mean by 'That is no problem …'?

We have reflected on why the practitioners in the nursery did not engage with this issue of such importance and interest to Jake and his family. Why did they seem to indicate that Jake and his dad's interest in his racial identity was a 'problem' when in fact Roberts-Holmes was sharing his pride in his child's drawings and conversations? Why did they not stop and listen as Jake's father offered what he had seen heard and noted at home of his son's ability to playfully and sensitively share his thinking about his own unique racial identity?

Did Jake's father just pick the wrong moment in the bustle of a nursery morning? Could it be that the practitioner who said 'That is no problem …' was embarrassed or lacking in confidence to talk about race? Was she being defensive as she was wary of inciting a racial incident or of causing offence to others? Did she in her heart believe that 'colour' does not matter? May be she was fearful of being accused of behaving in a racially prejudiced manner herself? Was she afraid of saying the 'wrong thing' or of being accused of not treating Jake equally or in a way that celebrated his differences as the only Black child in his class? Did she see differences as a bad thing in themselves? I wonder if Jake's father had brought in other aspects of Jake's talk or play from home, perhaps his interest in a book or his enthusiasm for a favourite toy, whether he would have had a similar dismissive response, or not?

As the staff seemed reluctant to engage in a dialogue about Jake's drawings that depicted different kinds of hair and his remarks about a variety of skin tones, could that be an instance of the adults unintentionally missing the opportunity to welcome and open up discussions on diversity?

If Jake and his family had had a Key Person who could have built up a rapport with them, and where key group times were a regular part of his day then there could have been more intimate opportunities to engage with the development of his racial identity.

However, if practitioners are not trained or have little understanding of issues of equalities then they will not have the knowledge or confidence to engage in this important aspect of their Key Person role. Increasingly what is *not* said rather than what *is* said or done may make Jake, and other mixed race children like him, feel that there is something unmentionable and 'wrong' about having curly hair and brown skin. Jake is at ease with this subject because of how it is freely discussed at home, but if it is not handled in the same way by his Key Persons in the nursery then it will not be long before his positive and confident racial identity will be eroded and he may say 'I wish I could be white like the other children', as we have witnessed in parallel situations.

This is a sample of the compelling evidence to support the Key Person role where understanding and empathy may be developed with parents from introductory meetings and home visits onwards. Key People will learn from their involvements with families how to handle differences confidently. They will have opportunities to rehearse what to say and how to talk about 'it', whether 'it' is a child's braided cornrows (a racial difference), a prosthetic limb (a child managing a disability), a child who screeches unexpectedly and unacceptably for what would be expected behaviour for the majority of the children (a child with autism), a child with a colostomy bag that needs changing (a child who needs specific caring for), a child who can play all the songs and rhymes by ear on the class piano (a gifted child) … or any other difference of one of the unique children in the group.

It is this kind of thinking, provoked by our relationships with key children in a group and supported by reflective discussion with mentors/supervisors and in staff meetings and professional development sessions, that that can help us to implement the EYFS statutory requirements and guidance:

> Look, listen and note young children's interest in similarities and differences … in physical appearance including hair texture and skin colour.
> (DfES, May 2008; Lane and Ouseley, 2010: 39)

> Talk with young children about valuing skin colour differences.
> (DfES, May 2008, Lane and Ouseley, 2010: 89)

Jake represented an example of one child in a specific setting. The following example is a study of how the home experiences of children from a poor and run-down urban area influences their transition from being a child in a family to being a pupil in school. This study exemplifies how the 'good intentions' of EYFS practitioners can sometimes allow children from certain backgrounds to become disaffected and fail within a school system that does not tune into *all* parents' cultural expectations, and children's culturally grounded learning experiences (Brooker, 2002). Brooker describes how in one school with a Bangladeshi and an 'Anglo' intake the children start school with very different literacy practices, opportunities and experiences from home.

The Bangladeshi children had been exposed to three alphabets (English, Bengali and Arabic) before starting school as well as having Sylheti as their first language. A few of the 'Anglo' children had started to learn letter sounds as well as letter names at home. Some children had used the local library since they were little while others had rarely seen a children's book before starting school. Some of the 'Anglo' children but none of the Bangladeshi group had a nightly bedtime story routine. All the Bangladeshi parents read the Qur'an and other prayer books every day with their children. Some Bangladeshi parents bought Bengali newspapers and discussed them in their family groups. Almost all the Bangladeshi families had Arabic tuition for their children and an hour or so was set aside for homework where little ones joined in with older siblings (Brooker, 2002: 37 and 57).

When Brooker (2002: 111) compared the starting school experiences of both groups of children three features emerged. First, children with homes that were like school accessed the toys, games and tasks far more easily. This was not easy for the children from Bangladeshi families. Second, the exchange of information was full and friendly with some of the 'Anglo' mothers who were at ease in the school but was harder for others more in awe of school protocol. Chatty exchanges were non-existent for most Bangladeshi Sylheti speaking mothers. Third, on entry assessments were unfair to children from minority cultures so there was a risk of children being seen, wrongly (as evidenced in this study), as unprepared for school learning.

This empathetic and insightful study of different families at home as well as in school reveals how unfair and unequal a child's chances of learning in school are likely to be unless EYFS practitioners go beyond cordial inviting smiles and kind-nesses and immerse themselves in the unfamiliar territory of cultures or class characteristics other than their own. This must be done if we are to build on the existing abilities of children as well as to sensitively introduce choices and materials that may be unfamiliar to them.

In effect, in this study, the researcher (Liz Brooker) took on some aspects of what a Key Person might do for the 16 children and their families as she visits and inter-viewed them in their homes and in their reception classroom over the year. She was able to be an advocate for them and a bridge between the class teachers and parents. She had many intimate conversations with the Bangldeshi parents over the year of the study as they learnt to trust her. Gradually they were able to express their disappoint-ments, worries, misunderstandings and disaffectedness with the education their children were receiving without fear of giving offence or feeling further excluded. Brooker was also able to communicate to the parents the rationale behind the peda-gogy of the play-based reception class so being a supporter and advocate of the school ethos and curriculum. This exemplifies how crucial for equality the Key Persons approach is in balancing things up for children from ethnic minorities as well as for some of the 'Anglo' families whose children had had impoverished language experi-ences before starting school.

All families express a keenness to support their children's education. However, in spite of affable and well-meaning relationships between EYFS practitioners and parents they will be less able to build on the literacy learning of children from back-grounds unlike their own unless each child and his/her family is assigned a Key Person – not only assigned a Key Person, but assigned one who is given time to build up a relationship of trust, confidence and mutual respect; a Key Person who is timetabled with 'non-contact times' so as to prepare for a new child and family in her/his group so that he/she can research for authentic knowledge of others heritages, languages, backgrounds or specific learning needs. This work may be needed for a *few* children in her key group.

So in practice there is still some way to go for all children to have an entitlement to a Key Person. The Key Persons approach should be a priority for settings and schools concerned about ensuring that practitioners and families really get to know each other. Building up trust and confidence between them faciltates a shared understanding of different cultural backgrounds and experiences that can help create a relationship where issues of racial equality may be freely raised and addressed (Lane, 2008).

Every practitioner who takes on the Key Person role with her small group will be likely to get to know families similar to their own and different from their own, families with different levels of education, different skin colours, different tastes and preferences, as well as other faiths or beliefs, cultural traditions and languages. Working with families who may have different opinions about child rearing and different emphasis on their ambitions and aspirations for their children in relation to the practitioner's own family children will be a challenge as well as a privilege. If Key Persons are able to create a rapport where they may be invited in, literally invited in on home visits, but also less literally into their hearts and minds then we can change the small communities of school as well as the wider community of neighbourhoods and make our polices on equality become more of a reality. When the Key Person is able to come alongside their small diverse group of assigned families then perhaps some of the sadness and frustrations of the examples I cited above can be avoided. New and life enhancing involvements in other families can develop for the Key People who invest that kind of selfless effort into acquiring new knowledge about how others live and what is important to them, however alien or 'other' that may seem at the beginning of the relationship.

Allocating children and their families to a Key Person

It is important to allocate a Key Person long before the children start in their settings and school so that each child may have an equal chance to learn and develop. We may plan for diverse social groups, from diverse families in each Key Persons group. This is a professional relationship of intimacy that is built up over time with support from the whole team as well as from mentors/managers. It is not about teaming all 'similar' children and families together, or clustering all Urdu speaking families with the teaching assistant who speaks that language, or offering all the children with Downs Syndrome to the teacher with a child with that condition in her family, for example. This is not a social gelling of who takes to whom. It is the beginning of a professional relationship with a small group of children and their families that is built up over time with opportunities for children, staff and families to get to know others similar to themselves as well as from different backgrounds (where that is possible with the children joining the group).

Guidelines for managers for implementing a Key Persons approach

This guidance for managers as they prepare for new enrolments is based on principles of *equality* for children, families and staff. These suggestions apply to the full age range but are added here as they are new to the second edition of this book and represent our experiences of working in settings and schools from 2003 to 2010 with practitioners who have worked to implement this approach. Further case studies and details of how others have implemented the Key Persons approach feature in the next chapter.

- Assign groups of children so as to build a mixed 'family' of children and parents from diverse backgrounds. This is in order to encourage children to be sensitive to the needs, views and feelings of others. There will be opportunities for developing respect for their own cultures, beliefs and backgrounds and those of other people. Openings can present themselves to begin to break down any learned prejudices, attitudes or behaviour.

- Assign children from the same family to the same Key Person when you can. If he/she has already worked with the family with older siblings she will already have established a relationship with the parents and can build on that experience. Twins should be in the same group for the same reason, though they may be better off in different groups for other assignments or teaching sessions.

- Where possible, give a smaller group of children to staff new to the role while they build up confidence and experience of working in this way.

- Plan to allocate staff to children who attend on the days they are working if they are not full time. Explain to parents the need to plan their working hours and take-up of places so that their Key Person can be as reliably available as is possible.

- Plan your staff training programme so that all practitioners have some Key Persons training to prepare them for taking on the role as well as opportunities for further professional development sessions to help them maintain relationships with a child and their family.

- Think about what support/mentoring strategies are in place before a practitioner is asked to take on the additional duties of the Key Person relationship.

- All staff are entitled to the opportunity and experience of developing their skills as a Key Person. It is a manager's role in the Key Persons approach to ensure all staff are not left out because they are more reserved, younger, less experienced, have less advanced qualifications, are new to the community or because they are 'other' or 'different' from the children and families in the group.

- Pair up an experienced Key Person with one newer to the task so that they may support each other.

- Where staff work in shifts or are the point of continuity between before and after school clubs, ensure this is a consideration in deciding which child should be in a Key Person's group.

- Plan for staff who are less outgoing to have time and support to build a relationship with their assigned families without the more sociable or confident staff members taking over the interactions. The assigned pairings need time and space to nurture the bonds of an attachment relationship.

- Ensure the Key Person is one of the staff who visits the child and family at home. This is a vital step in beginning a relationship for a family who chooses to welcome this kind of visit.

- Think about the balance of the group when allocating a child to a Key Person's group. Do not overwhelm her by assigning all the children most likely to have difficulty in settling, or for whom English is a second language, or from impoverished backgrounds or from families with mental health/illness problems, for example, to the same group.

- Assign each child to a group where they can learn new ways of being. They may learn some words of another language, develop close friendships with children who may have a different skin tone, build alliances with children from a different part of town, have chances to help children who are less mobile than themselves, and so on.

- As a manager, take responsibility for assigning children rather than being drawn into parent requests or staff preferences for the most 'popular' pairings of Key Person and child. It is important not to wait until after the child starts to see who gels with whom. This may create imbalance and unintentional staff contention, unequal professional opportunities and demands. Some of us are more outgoing and gregarious, or may be familiar with children from home contacts. This can lead to 'Mary Poppins/Pied Piper' led choices for a Key Person from parents. Preferences from the staff may be expressed as they seek to be the Key person with their friend's children. That said, of course this could be one of the considerations to take into account after paying heed to all the criteria for assigning children to a Key Person set out here.

- Some children entering your group may be known to you from taster visits or from when they have been part of other groups or sessions associated with your centre, school or setting. The child may express a preference for a particular member of staff. It is an important consideration to take account of the voice of the child where possible in allocating their Key Person. This decision needs to be weighed up in relation to all the above points.

The Key Persons approach in practice

Strategies for getting started and organised in primary schools and pre-schools

Issues for:

Reception class teachers and teaching assistants with:		Practitioners in pre-schools with:
■ early years coordinators; ■ head teachers/senior management team; ■ EYFS governors/PTA; ■ supporting EYFS advisory teachers and consultants.	and	■ pre-school leaders; ■ owners and/or business managers ■ 'head office' for private nursery companies; ■ parent committee members/PTA; ■ supporting EYFS advisory teachers and consultants.

Before implementing a Key Persons approach there are many issues that need to be discussed with the whole settings and school team, and in particular with managers/head teachers. Considering these issues when planning and organising helps the EYFS staff get the support that they will need from managers and may ensure that everyone understands the importance of this approach.

Here are some starting points for these discussions:

■ What do EYFS teachers, teaching assistants, and pre-school practitioners need to read and what **induction and training** is there to introduce them to the theory and practice of a Key Persons approach (KPA)? Government programmes such as Social and Emotional Aspects of Development and Every Child a Talker may support the professional development programmes for a Key Persons approach. (Some of the case studies in the next chapter show what other practitioners have read and training that they found to be important.) The references in this book offer many opportunities for introductory and further reading.

■ How soon can the school/setting ensure that there are **full-time designated staff** in the nursery and reception classes so that it becomes possible to begin to implement a Key Persons approach? In reception classes this approach will need a *minimum* of one full-time teacher and one full-time teaching assistant to 30 children in this infant class so that there are two Key Persons with two groups. Looking ahead to a ratio of 1:10 would mean each Key Person would have a better chance of forming a relationship of 'professional intimacy' (Elfer, 1996) and attachment (Geddes, 2006) with their group of children and their families. Many primary schools will already have teaching assistants or nursery nurses appointed to the reception class as established good practice (DCSF, 2007b: para 3.24: 18).

In nursery settings there needs to be a core of full-time staff for similar reasons. Will this require deployment changes in your setting to be managed by owners/leaders/'head office' over time to ensure each child does not experience serial short-term assigned Key People who will not have adequate time to build attachment relationships?

- How will settings and school **development plans** document the steps and time line for the introduction of a Key Persons approach, with its associated requirements for **funding, staffing, training, support and mentoring** for staff taking on the Key Person role?

- How can the early years coordinator and settings and school managers work towards forming an integrated **Early Years Foundation Stage Unit**? This is when the reception class joins with the nursery class or pre-school setting so as to avoid unnecessary transitions of Key Persons and the damaging experiences for children of '*serial carers*' (Selleck, 2006b).

- When can reception class staff meet with the **EYFS governor/parent representative** and the primary school team who will need to be informed about the theory and practice of the Key Persons approach developing in the reception class so that they may enlist their support and involvement with whole school planning?

- How will the settings and school develop **strategies for informing and involving the parents** in the development of a Key Persons approach so as to establish this way of working as part of the school's ethos? What does it say about your Key Person policy in your prospectus, welcome pack, parent notice board, or newsletter? What opportunities do parents have to discuss the relationship? Are there opportunities for parents representatives to share or discuss their experiences of the Key Person relationship with parents new to the settings and school?

- What can you do to prepare for an **Ofsted inspection**? If you are not yet ready to take on the Key Persons approach in your school or setting (because ratios, staffing, training plans, etc. are yet to be implemented), think about what inspectors will need to know so that they may appreciate the steps being taken towards developing this approach and the barriers blocking working in this way.

- It is important that Key Persons, at **key group times**, ensure that the main focus is about **developing close relationships**. When can children expect their Key Person to be predictably accessible, affectionate, responsive and sensitive, in an encounter together that is tailor-made for them? How can lead reception class teachers counter any pressures for key times to be eclipsed by adult-led teaching targets, standards or assessments? What can they offer their colleagues so they will understand that key group times with their key children are for authentic reciprocal conversations that are personal and matched to each unique child's experiences? What times will you put into the weekly routine and which places can you organise so that children may have regular informal encounters with their Key Person and the other children in the small group?

- How will the lead reception class teacher/pre-school leader ensure that each (full time) EYFS practitioner who will be taking on the role of Key Person can prepare and get to know his/her assigned group of children and their families before they join the reception class/group? When would it be best to arrange for

planning and preparation time for each Key Person so they can meet with a child's Key Persons from previous settings – as well as the families of their group of key children? When may preparation and planning time for researching and developing materials to take account of the culture and contribution of each family take place?

■ How can Key Person practitioners prepare to be a Key Person for **children in families similar to their own as well as different from their own**? How may they support and sustain the development of each child's ethnic, cultural, religious, social and family background as well as introducing them to this new aspect of their lives – that of becoming a pupil in the school? What help, information, training, resources or useful web sites can managers/head teachers offer to people taking on the Key Person role with families with a background that is new to them?

■ What is the best way to ensure Key People have **regular support and mentoring**, separate from appraisal or target-setting, so that there is time to talk about the attachment relationships that are being developed with children and families? How will the reception class teacher prepare the teaching assistants or nursery nurses to get ready for their role and support them to embrace this new opportunity to be in a special relationship with a few of the children in the class and their families? Who will take on the mentoring role? How often can these sessions be organised? Does your school/setting have a place for these meetings to be uninterrupted? What training do managers need to take on mentoring, if this is a new aspect of their leadership role?

■ How might **Key Person pairs** be established to ensure that families and children can rely on their Key Person – or the back-up person – being reliably accessible even when there are staff away for training or because of sickness? What thought may be given to ensure **supply teachers/agency staff** are already known to the children and that there is as much continuity as possible when there are unavoidable extended absences of Key Person staff? How will supply/agency staff be informed about the Key Persons approach and prepared for their part in working with the EYFS staff team in this way? How will they reassure children – and their parents – that their Key Person has not 'abandoned' them? How might Key Persons stay in touch and reassure that they are keeping each other in mind during unavoidable separations?

■ How will the Key Person **contribute observations** for each of the children in their group to inform planning and assessment and to be an advocate for them? How will their professionally intimate relationships ensure that activities can be introduced or extended to build on each child's experiences and interests? What links will there be with the Key Person and the lead teacher/practitioner responsible for curriculum planning and assessments for the class/group?

■ As leader of the EYFS team in a reception class or nursery group, how will you ensure that everyone, including **staff who are not Key Persons** (e.g. supply teachers, part-time staff, job-share pairs, students, lunchtime supervisors, parent helpers, resident artists, music and dance specialists, etc.) understand the importance of supporting each child's attachment to their Key Person? How will you encourage each child to have time with all the adults who bring new opportunities and experiences for learning while ensuring that the adults who are not Key Persons know when to hand over to the child's Key Person for intimate physical care, when children need comforting at times of stress – or containment at times when they are struggling to regulate their emotions?

■ And finally – how will you **plan for and manage the ending of the Key Person relationship** with a child and their family? What will you do – or keep – or hand back to the child? What will you do for parents to say goodbye and mark the ending of the professional bond you have established? Sometimes it is inevitable – however much we work to ensure that children have a continuous relationship with their Key Persons throughout the EYFS this is not always possible at the moment within our present system. So what will you need to do to manage the transition to the new Key Person assigned to the child? This may be the unavoidable transition to another room or class or when they must move on to another EYFS setting or school. Last, but definitely not least, how will you let go of the special professional intimacy of your attachment to your key children when they move on? This work of ending is as important as the work of preparing and establishing the special relationship at the beginning. How will you keep the memories of these children safe? What may you keep? What does the school/setting need to keep? In what circumstances and with whose permissions do we gather our own scrap books, memory boxes or records of children who have been special for us? What support can mentors give to ending the Key Person relationship? What responsibility do mentors have for overseeing these endings so that they may support Key People to establish professional boundaries and limits to this relationship? How will you – as a Key Person – celebrate the special part you played as a Key Person in the child's well-being, positive self identity, mental health, learning and friendships in their formative early years?

And finally …

… implementing a Key Persons approach is a journey, not a destination.

We have offered some practical steps on the journey for creating the professional ethos from which a Key Persons approach may emerge, so that settings and schools have some of the support and access to information they need to get started. However, we must emphasise that no strategy or arrangement can ensure a Key Persons approach. It is only people building relationships with people – that is, the triangle of trust between a Key Person, the child and their family supported over time by skilled mentors so as to reflect on those relationships – that will enhance the well-being, mental health, learning and equal chances for all the children in the second half of the EYFS. Many early years settings, and most reception class staff, will be at the beginning of this journey at the time of publication and will have much to learn from their EYFS colleagues working with babies and the younger children where the Key Persons approach may have been established for some time.

The Key Person journey
Its benefits and challenges

In this last chapter we return to one of our main messages of this book – the idea of the Key Persons approach as a continuing journey of professional endeavour and determination in respectful partnership with children and family members. We think the essence of the approach is about holding onto the importance for children of feeling emotionally safe and secure, individually thought about and responded to. We regard this as the basis for all else each child might be and become, in the early years setting, and in what they take with them beyond nursery.

The chapter is made up of a series of 18 case studies or vignettes about the Key Persons approach and its implementation in different kinds of setting. We are enormously grateful to the practitioners and writers who have shared these accounts with us. We hope you will read them in the spirit with which they were given to us, as open, honest reflections of progress on the particular journeys these setting are making. We deliberately asked for accounts that show the difficulties and challenges of the work as well as the benefits and achievements because we believe that is the reality of working with a Key Persons approach. The aim of presenting them here is to illustrate some of these benefits and challenges but also to serve as a kind of testimony to the challenges of the approach and the need for a continual stance of mutual, constructively critical, support and appraisal.

The examples are selected on the basis that they each demonstrate the sense of a journey in implementing the Key Persons approach. They are not included as 'models' of good practice to be simply replicated. Indeed, we hope they will be critiqued but in a way that honours the integrity and effort that has been invested in the professional work they describe.

We have divided the examples into four themes:

A   Establishing the Key Persons approach.
B   The importance of continuity of Key Persons through the early years setting and into Key Stage 1.
C   The impact of the Key Persons approach.
D   Maintaining the Key Persons approach when it is established.

We have not added any commentary about the examples but hope they will stimulate reflection in discussion about how the Key Persons approach is established, its impact and how some of the challenges can be met.

Theme A: Establishing the Key Persons approach

Example 1: From key worker system to Key Persons approach – creating foundations (Debra Laxton, Lecturer, Chichester College of Further Education and former Key Person, Chichester Children's Centre)

I am sure the reader will agree that it is often easier to see things objectively as an outsider. In this case I was the outsider; a college lecturer working to gain early years professional status, carrying out a placement in the baby room of a large 140-place nursery on a college campus.

The staff within the room were hard working, keen and committed to delivering the best possible care for the children. Each staff member was a key worker, allocated specific children to plan and maintain records for. During the day all practitioners randomly took on various roles to meet the children's needs. On early shifts the nearest available adult welcomed parents and children into the setting over a low fence which ensured infant security. Infants were passed across from parent to practitioner with parents rarely coming through the gate. Nappies and bottle feeds were carried out on a rota basis and at mealtimes children were supported by a number of different practitioners. Children in need of comfort were responded to by the nearest staff member and at the end of the day parents were greeted by those on the late shift.

The manager had become concerned that children were reliant on one particular adult and became distressed when their Key Person was absent. To address this, the manager informed staff that the care of children should be shared, to avoid close relationships developing and so prevent unnecessary anxiety.

Having been a Key Person and knowing the benefits of the approach, I was keen to instigate a review of the way the old 'key worker system' was operating within this room. The first step was a sensitively led discussion with the manager where empathy was shown regarding the difficulty of staffing long days, covering staff sickness and holidays. Evidence was then provided that demonstrated the importance of developing a genuine bond with children (DfES, 2007: card 2.4) and the difference a secure base can make (Bowlby, 1988). The concept of 'back up' Key Person to support children through shift patterns and staff leave was explained and the manager responded positively, inviting me to lead a discussion on the subject at the monthly staff meeting.

At this meeting the hard work and commitment of practitioners was acknowledged and they were encouraged to consider how their practice could be improved in line with current evidence. Government guidance (EYFS) and key components from attachment theory research were shared, alongside my own positive experience as a Key Person. Some staff described a sense of relief that it was appropriate and in the best interest of the child to develop close relationships. Others had valid questions about the practicalities of implementing the approach. These issues were discussed constructively with staff reacting positively to suggested changes regarding moving from a *key worker system* to a *Key Persons approach*, and were quick to create buddy teams that would better support children physically and through paired planning to improve effectiveness, and meal times were reorganised to allow for key grouping.

The complexity of implementing the Key Persons approach should not be underestimated. In this case the single aspect of time, which can be mistakenly considered a simple factor, created a variety of challenges. The change from key worker system to Key Persons approach was implemented near the end of the work placement because it was necessary to take time to discover areas of weakness within the setting and to establish myself as an approachable, competent and knowledgeable practitioner that staff could trust and go to for advice and support. It was essential to take the time to listen to the staff individually and offer constructive advice so improvements would be successful and sustainable. This process ensured staff were engaged and not left feeling criticised and demoralised. Once the old key worker system had been highlighted as a project for improvement it was important to be patient, once again, and wait until the monthly staff meeting to introduce the topic.

The instigation of the review was only a starting point and it was difficult to withdraw at the end of the placement with the approach still in the inception phase, however it was important to allow the setting to take ownership of the approach and make developments based on the needs of its children, staff and parents. Essential to the success of the Key Persons approach is an agreed philosophy with principles and aims that provide a structure for implementation, facilitating consistent practice and parental involvement across the setting. In the above scenario substantial changes were initiated without conflict. However, practice change needs to be consistently evaluated and issues responded to so that the value of the approach is fully realised by children, their carers and childcare practitioners.

Valuable lessons were learnt from this experience and these will be briefly examined. It is beneficial to reflect objectively on practice or invite someone you trust to offer constructive criticism. As an experienced practitioner on a short-term placement it was relatively easy to observe objectively whilst building a rapport with staff and I felt accepted as a critical friend. Valuing what teams already offer is important and in this case staff in the baby room had demonstrated, both verbally and through their actions, a commitment to wanting to do the best for the children in their care. This was something to communicate back to the staff and offered a starting point by suggesting that such dedicated practitioners would be keen to reflect on their practice and look for ways to develop. This established a positive working relationship and staff were open to suggestions, ready to be motivated and keen to provide innovative ideas about how they could further enrich children's lives through the Key Persons approach. The success of this strategy emphasised the significance of listening to those with first-hand experience.

A month after the initial changes had been made, a list of suggested tasks that should be part of the role of the Key Person was used for discussion with room leaders. The list enabled developments to be recognised whilst highlighting further areas for improvement and deciding on future actions. Such actions included developing an awareness of their communication with young children; initially practitioners were to take note of their interactions with key children during nappy changes and consider how this could be improved. Staff discussions supported progress and use of gestures and voice tone were seen as areas all staff could use more effectively throughout the day. The list provided a useful tool for collaborative working that allowed staff to plan agreed achievable goals; without this, failure was more likely.

Once all staff were aware of the Key Persons approach it was fundamental to inform and involve parents. The nursery was given suggestions of how this could be successful, and ideas included a display in the reception area, producing a leaflet for the new children welcome pack, offering an information evening for parents and informal discussions with parents by the Key Persons during drop off or collection times. This communication would give parents the opportunity to share their perspective as the children's main carers and they too could have innovative ideas of how to improve practice.

The Key Persons approach was set to be part of future monthly staff meetings and the deputy manager, who had demonstrated a keen interest in supporting the development of the approach, was eager to follow up changes and lead progress reports and discussions. Positive points brought to the meeting were that transitions from one room to another had been eased, with children settling more easily and staff enjoying the closer contact with key children. Challenges were organisational issues concerned with shift patterns and trying to organise paired buddy teams where there were five members of staff in the room. Giving staff the chance to exchange views in a safe, open and honest way allowed for shared achievements and working together to find solutions that may not solve the problem completely but could provide some improvement. It is essential to make time for a cycle of reflection where practitioners are encouraged to share their views and concerns to allow for continuous improvement of the Key Persons approach and these staff meetings gave the time and opportunity for the nursery staff to do this.

Example 2: Establishing the Key Persons approach in a reception class (Sue Harris, Advisory Teacher Oxfordshire County Council)

This is an example of home visits carried out by reception class teacher Liz Riches at Queensway Primary School in Banbury. Sue Harris, the advisory teacher, supported her work by making a video of the visits. She talked to the parents with the staff in the school to introduce them to the Key Persons approach and wrote this account of their ongoing Key Persons journey in July 2010.

To develop the Key Persons approach in the reception class of a one entry class primary school, the foundation stage teacher and her full-time teaching assistant assign each child to a key adult, and for part of their induction policy have introduced home visits.

At an induction meeting in the school for prospective new children and their families they are asked if they would be happy to receive a visit from the class teacher. All the families agreed to a visit. The class teacher is able to work with the local outreach worker from the local Children's Centre to arrange two days to make the visits.

The visits are organised by the class teacher who confirms a time with each family. On the visit she takes a small gift of a canvas bag with a note pad and pencil for the child and further leaflets and information about local drop-in facilities for parents and their children. She also has her own bag with a few toys from the classroom and a selection of books to look at. The visit may include introductions, talking about induction days, and arrangements for the first day. The Key Person may share the toys with the child and can read a story chosen by the child. She will take a photograph that will be used to display in the classroom. The Key Person will also show the child her ID badge with her own photograph on it. The visiting staff can then answer any questions the parents may have and begin to build a relationship with them.

A while after the visits the teacher gave a questionnaire to parents to collate their thoughts on the home visits. Overall everyone welcomed the opportunity of a home visit and felt it had a positive impact on their children starting school.

The Key Person team now see many advantages to introducing home visit as their first steps to a Key Persons approach:

- The staff meet the parents and children in a familiar, comfortable environment.
- Families have the opportunity to talk confidentially to their Key Person.
- Children can meet their Key Person on a one-to-one basis and start to build trust in her.
- The foundation stage team have a fuller picture of life at home, family situations and other key adults.
- Working with the outreach worker strengthens links with Children's Centre staff.
- The foundation stage staff have an opportunity to note the learning environment at home, e.g. access to books and toys, cooking, gardening activities.
- The Key Person can be a role model for positive interactions, reading a story together, talking about the local park – this is important in this school where many children may have had fewer opportunities for play and talk with adults.
- On two occasions a video was taken to document the visit, reflect on practice and use for training. Copies were given to the families for their own photograph library.

The challenges of this approach were:

- making time to arrange the visits and finding cover for class in school;
- arranging for an additional adult to accompany the visits;
- finding time for the teaching assistant as well as the teacher to visit her key children;
- trying not to make judgements in homes that are very different from your own;
- establishing strategies to cope with children who are not willing or unable to interact with the teacher.

The next three examples represent the Manchester Buddy project 2010, which was designed to introduce the Key Persons approach to primary school foundation stage classes. This project was led by Mary Lestrange, Quality Assurance Officer at Manchester Sure Start Children's Services. An early years setting was paired with a school to develop early years practice and to promote the principle that the Key Persons approach 'sits at the heart of early years practice'. This work is ongoing but these following case studies report on the progress made after the first year into their Key Persons journey, supported with resources for training and reference reading material by local authority officers.

Example 3: Developing the Key Persons approach in Rupert's Day Nursery (Sharon Meade, Manager)

TABLE 5.1 Grouping of children

	NUMBER OF CHILDREN	NUMBER OF STAFF WITH ROLE
Room: babies	6	2
Room: toddlers	9	3
Room: tweenies	12	3
Room: pre-school	16	2

How have you developed the Key Persons approach in your setting?

At Rupert's we first engaged with the Key Persons approach when becoming involved with a project called Intimacy Island. The idea behind this was to ensure important key times were provided to each child to be with her Key Person and to be able to express her personal feelings and have a voice within her learning development. After the success of this project the staff and myself were very willing to move forward to improve our provision again and became involved in the Budding Project with Sandilands School to look at the role of the Key Person through transitions that our children have to encounter when leaving our setting to attend a school setting.

Each child at Rupert's Day Nursery on induction has a Key Person to provide for them and their family's needs throughout their time with us. Within each unit each Key Person has a secondary Key Person who will assist them and work closely with them to plan for the needs of the children they are caring for. The ratio for the under 2s unit is one to three and therefore the staff are easily available to assist all their children in their learning and development. The over 2s unit is a mixture of children between the ages of 2 and 5 and the ratios vary from one to four to one to eight within the foundation stage unit.

We decided to focus initially upon the transition from home to nursery then to the pre-school setting into school. The induction to the nursery is very flexible at Rupert's and the child/parent or carer are invited to attend a number of settling in visits to assist in the settling of the child and the introduction of their Key Person. During the first initial weeks the Key Person develops a profile of the child's daily visits and the parent's comments on the settling experience. This enables the parents, child and the Key Person to begin to build positive relationships. Key information is exchanged and the Key Person also provides the child and parents with an information sheet all about themselves to help develop the relationship.

We arrange children's starting dates so that no more than one new child starts on each day; this helps to ensure that their Key Person has quality time to spend with them and their parents to help get them settled.

When moving onto a school setting, children who had previously attended the same pre-school were placed with the same Key Person at the school and started school at a similar time.

We have worked with Sandilands School to develop transition activities. For example, through the buddying project Goldilocks and the three bears puppets were purchased and used by the Key Person and their child. At Rupert's these experiences were recorded within a big floor book and then used at Sandilands as well; this helped to promote recognition of resources within both settings for the child. A CD containing a short Powerpoint presentation showing photographs of the Key Persons at Sandilands and the new environment was given to ourselves so that we could prepare our children for their next environment. Both children and their Key Person watched the DVD and any questions that arose were recorded in the big floor book. A book about 'my special people' was developed in both settings between each Key Person, parents/carers and the child to help the child feel more secure about moving and that their old Key Person was not just cut from their life but still a part of the new transition. This enabled their new Key Person to have a starting point and to spend quality time with their child and to add their photograph to the book which would help to aid in starting conversations with the child.

Our observation and assessment procedures enable the Key Person to have responsibility for observing their children and to plan for their next steps in learning and development. Each Key Person has dedicated time to observe their children and to undertake activities targeted at their learning and development needs. The Key Person also encourages parents/carers to make contributions to their children's learning journeys/portfolios and lead the discussions during parental consultations or meetings.

At Rupert's we ensure that our children's personal care procedures, wherever possible, are with their Key Person, e.g. nappy changing, washing hands, mealtimes, etc.

We noticed that it was at the beginning of the day that children seemed less emotionally secure and realised that this was an important time for everyone. We spoke to parents about this situation and we have now rearranged timings and rotas to ensure that wherever possible a child always has their Key Person or secondary Key Person around at these times. We took photographs of the parents handing over their child to their Key Person and made a parent book for the children to sit and look at if they became distressed, and the Key Person would then talk with them about any emotions they were feeling and reassure them that this was ok .

As part of the buddying project we have also been looking at how we can further develop the role of the Key Person to enhance personal and social skills. We have dedicated group time every day for the Key Person to meet with their group in a special place and to undertake activities that are planned to develop these skills. Wherever possible, it is the Key Person who also helps children resolve any conflicts that may arise throughout the day through reasoning and talk. We also use empathy dolls at both Rupert's and Sandilands, which help children develop emotional literacy.

At Rupert's the children have developed personalities for our dolls. 'Tom' is a little shy and unsure of his environment and he gets upset within big open spaces – he likes quiet little corners to explore and develop, he doesn't like shouting or loud noises. He likes to talk quietly and likes his friends to listen to him. 'Nina' loves noise especially music and likes to dance all the time but she doesn't like to share very much and wants to keep all the musical toys to herself. The children problem-solve different ways to help Nina to share.

What are the responsibilities of the Key Person (e.g. support transitions, compile Learning Journeys, and take care of personal needs)?

- build close secure relationships with the child;
- support the child in new situations (e.g. transitions);
- build relationships with parents and try to remove any barriers to engagement;
- make incidental along with detailed observations and assessments of children;
- work with other Key People to identify and plan for children's developmental and learning needs;
- play alongside children, be creative/engage in sustained shared thinking;
- share information with parents regarding children's next steps in learning;
- have special key group times and places;
- help children to resolve any conflicts through reasoning and talk;
- create and contribute to children's learning journeys;
- provide information to aid the tracking of children's progress;
- attend to children's personal needs wherever possible;
- inform other practitioners of important information that they need to know regarding children (e.g. health needs, special preferences, interests);
- provide information to other agencies regarding a child, and if needed assist in development plans;
- raise concerns about a child's development and assist in providing the help they need.

Do you provide any key group times throughout the day or week (e.g. meeting and greeting, snack times, lunchtime)?

At Rupert's we have set times throughout the day where there are planned activities for children to work in smaller groups this is where they will discuss certain topics that are relevant to their learning, for example their own planning and preferences, maybe new children settling, the effects of new babies at home, etc. Children also meet individually with their Key Person. For example, in the morning as parent's drop off their child each Key Person will spend one-to-one time to settle the child into an activity or interest of theirs to help them begin their day. Also individual time is spent when the Key Person and the child work on their individual portfolios (e.g. placing photos in and writing any comments made).

At lunchtime key groups sit together with their Key Person and enjoy meals together and discuss healthy eating. They work as a team when setting up or clearing up after lunch.

What training has been accessed to support the role (e.g. attachment theory, supporting PSED, Key Persons approach)?

Mary Lestrange (Practise Development Officer) and Anne Crocker (Children's Centre Teacher) provided training to the setting regarding the Key Persons role. Staff from Rupert's also attended further joint training at Sandilands School to discuss the importance of the child's portfolio's and the Key Person.

Training on attachment theory was delivered and led by Martin Carey. He helped the practitioners to look deeper at the behaviours and responses of the children.

Through the buddying project, several books have been purchased for reading and these have been used as a stimulus for improving practice discussions. Different ways to assist in the learning and development of children have been explored.

What impact have the changes had on children, families, staff and setting?

The staff have given their full commitment to this project and they value their importance, with having a more defined role with a particular group of children. They feel that they know the children in their group much better now and are therefore able to respond to their needs more readily and sensitively. It also helps when looking to support the children in their next steps of development and in any transitions they have to encounter. When reporting to parents at the end of the day the staff can be confident of delivering a personal touch and evaluation on their key children, as all information about a child is fed directly back to their Key Person.

Many parents value the input and support each morning from their child's Key Person and they have built strong working relationships together. Parents have said that they feel reassured knowing that one particular person is taking extra special care of their child.

Due to the involvement of the Key Person during the transition visits, when parents and children visit their new school we have now developed a new beginning of a positive relationship between old and new Key Persons for each child. I feel that some of the barriers that parents feel about school have diminished considerably; also we are building a new working relationship to join both settings together to focus on the needs of the child.

The parents of children that have moved to Sandilands have said that the home visits have really enabled the Key Person to get to know the child in an environment that they are familiar and comfortable in. Many children refer to the time that their Key Person came and played at their house!

Although rearranging rotas to ensure that a Key Person has quality time to spend with their key children has been challenging at times and required flexibility in routines, it has been well worth the effort as the vast majority of children now settle quicker and readily turn to their Key Person for support when needed. Partnerships with parents have improved and they now leave for work settled with the knowledge that their children are happy at play.

We are really starting to see the benefits of the Key Person dealing with children's personal and social issues, with children responding well. The children now feel they have a voice and their opinions and decisions they make are valued. They understand that it is ok to express different feelings within different situations they come across.

Developing the role of the Key Person within this area has been a challenge, but one that the whole team has risen to. Key People feel more empowered within their work, parents are more engaged with the development of their children and children happier that they are truly listened to!

Example 4: Developing the Key Persons approach in Sandilands Primary School (Lorraine Brooks – was Foundation Stage Leader at the school – now teacher at Sure Start in Manchester)

TABLE 5.2 Grouping of children

	NUMBER OF CHILDREN	NUMBER OF STAFF WITH ROLE
Nursery	60	5
Reception	47	4
Foundation stage unit	107	9

How have you developed the Key Persons approach in your setting?

We have been involved in the buddying project with Rupert's day nursery and together we have been looking at ways to develop the role of the Key Person.

Each 'class' of children at Sandilands has one teacher and at least one teaching assistant who work closely together to plan for the needs of the children. Teachers and teaching assistants are the Key Person for no more than 13 children each. Children in the whole of the Foundation Stage have a Key Person and a secondary Key Person that they can turn to if their Key Person is away.

We focused initially upon the transition from home/pre-school setting into school. We offered parents a home visit by their child's prospective Key Person before their child started school. The home visits were a huge success. The parents, child and Key Person began to build positive relationships even before the child started school. Key information was exchanged and the Key Person also provided the child and parents with an information sheet all about themselves to help develop the relationship.

We arranged the starting dates so that no more than two new children started each day and rotas were adjusted so that their Key Person had quality time to spend with them and their parents to get them settled. Children who had previously attended the same pre-school were placed with the same Key Person and started at a similar time.

We have worked with Rupert's day nursery to develop transition activities. For example, through the Buddying project Goldilocks and the three bears puppets were purchased and used by the Key Person and child first at Rupert's and then at Sandilands. A CD containing a short Powerpoint presentation showing photographs of the Key People at Sandilands and the new environment was also given to settings that children were coming from.

The Key Person for each child has worked with parents to collect photographs of people that are special to them – including their previous and present Key Person wherever possible. The Key Person has then spent quality time with each of their children compiling very special books for them to share.

To further develop the role of the Key Person we have also introduced stay and play sessions each morning to enable the Key Person and parents to have some quality time to interact, share information and talk about the children's next steps in learning.

We have recently changed our observation and assessment procedures to give the Key Person greater responsibility for observing their children and helping the teachers to plan for their next steps in learning. Each Key Person now has dedicated time to observe their children and to undertake activities targeted at their learning and development needs. The Key Person also makes a major contribution to the children's Learning Journeys and during parental consultations.

We have changed our personal care procedures to ensure that wherever possible it is the Key Person who changes children when necessary.

We noticed that it was at lunchtime that children seemed less emotionally secure and we realised that it was often because their Key Person was not there for them. We have now rearranged timings and rotas to ensure that wherever possible a child always has their Key Person or secondary Key Person around at lunch times!

As part of the buddying project we have also been looking at how we can further develop the role of the Key Person to enhance personal and social skills. We now have dedicated group time every day for the Key Person to meet with their group and undertake activities that are planned to develop these skills (e.g. circle time). Wherever possible, it is the Key Person who also helps children resolve any conflicts that may arise throughout the day through reasoning and talk. We also plan to use empathy dolls at both Rupert's and Sandilands to help children develop emotional literacy.

What are the responsibilities of the Key Person?

- build close secure relationships with the child;
- support the child in new situations (e.g. transitions);
- build relationships with parents and try to remove any barriers to engagement;
- make incidental and detailed observations of children;
- work with teachers to identify and plan for children's developmental and learning needs;
- play alongside children/engage in sustained shared thinking;

- share information with parents regarding children's next steps in learning;
- have special group times;
- help children to resolve any conflicts through reasoning and talk;
- contribute to children's Learning Journeys;
- provide information to aid the tracking of children's progress;
- attend to children's personal needs wherever possible;
- inform other practitioners of important information that they need to know regarding children (e.g. health needs);
- provide information to concerned agencies regarding a child;
- raise concerns about a child.

Do you provide any key group times throughout the day or week?

At Sandilands, children of nursery age meet with their Key Person at least four times a day:

- at 9.15 after the stay and play session;
- at 11.15 before dinner;
- at 1.00pm after dinner;
- at 2.30 before home time.

Children of reception age meet with their Key Person at least twice a day, at 9.15 am and 2.30pm. The other group sessions that they have are developmentally grouped for communication, language and literacy development (CLLD) and problem solving, reasoning and numeracy (PSRN).

Throughout the week there is always planned time for children to work in even smaller groups, or individually with their Key Person.

There is a special group time on Fridays where the children reflect on the things that they have been doing that week (aided with photographs) and plan with their Key Person the things that they would like to do the following week.

What training has been accessed to support the role (attachment theory, supporting PSED, Key Persons approach)?

There has been whole foundation staff training led by Mary Lestrange (Practice Development Officer) and Anne Crocker (Children's Centre Teacher) regarding the Key Person role. There has also been training on attachment led by Martin Carey.

Along with this, through the buddying project, several books have been purchased for reading and these have been used as a stimulus for improving practise discussions.

What impact have the changes had on children, families, staff and school?

Due to the involvement of the Key Person during the home visits, when parents and children enter school, a positive relationship has already begun. I feel that some of the barriers to parental involvement in school have diminished considerably. Many parents stay and play each morning and have built strong working relationships with their child's Key Person. Parents have said that they feel reassured knowing that one particular person is taking extra special care of their child – especially as Sandiland's is such a large environment.

The home visits have really enabled the Key Person to get to know the child in an environment that they are familiar and comfortable in. Many children refer to the time that their Key Person came and played at their house!

Although rearranging rotas to ensure that a Key Person has quality time to spend with their new children has been challenging at times and required flexibility in routines, it has been well worth it as the vast majority of new children have settled quickly and readily turn to their Key Person for support when needed.

The Key Persons have said that they really enjoy having a more defined role with a particular group of children. They feel that they know the children in their group much better now and are therefore able to respond to their needs more readily and sensitively. It also helps when reporting to parents at the end of the day, as all information about a child is fed directly back to their Key Person.

We are really starting to see the benefits of the Key Person dealing with children's personal and social issues, with children responding well.

Developing the role of the Key Person has been a challenge, but one that the whole team has risen to. Key Persons feel more empowered, parents are more engaged and children happier!

Example 5: Developing the Key Persons approach in Crumpsall Primary School (Paula Cassidy, Teaching Assistant)

TABLE 5.3 Grouping of children

	NUMBER OF CHILDREN	NUMBER OF STAFF WITH ROLES
Nursery	39	1 teacher
		1 TA level 2
		1 TA level 3
Reception	60	2 teachers
		2 TA level 2

How have you developed the Key Persons approach in your setting?

The school has been involved in the Manchester Buddying Project, which aimed to 'buddy' early years settings and schools together, sharing best practice around developing the role of the Key Person.

The group began by developing a Key Person audit which was then completed by the Foundation stage practitioners in order to reflect on their current practice and to identify a focus for future development. Parent questionnaires were also used to gain an insight into parents' awareness of the Key Person role, and to explore how parents felt about the relationships they had with their children's practitioners.

Training opportunities, buddy group meetings and reflection on action sessions provoked thought and discussion on how routines and daily practice could be organised to ensure children's emotional needs were being supported.

For the first time children were allocated a Key Person in nursery before they actually started. This allowed the children and their families to become familiar with their Key Person during visits, and the Key Person to begin building a relationship with the family. Children will remain in these mixed age and ability key groups throughout nursery in order for them to develop warm, trusting relationships where the Key Person supports children to feel good about themselves and be confident and ready to play and learn.

Each key group has their own 'special' carpet area. Children easily identify with their area, as photos of them and their Key Person are displayed alongside examples of their work. On arrival in the morning children gather in their key groups and self-register with the support of their Key Person.

A great opportunity for reflection was opened up by video recording particular times of day. We decided to capture how available we were to parents at the beginning and end of the school day, as we were acutely aware of how important developing relationships with parents is, if the Key Persons approach is to be successful. A number of changes were implemented as a result of this exercise, such as the foundation stage opening its doors ten minutes before school starts to encourage parents to come in and settle their children or talk to the Key Person, who is always on hand. Parents are now welcomed into the classrooms five minutes before the end of school day also. This has proved so successful that the whole school now follow this routine.

Continuing to develop ways of working in partnership with parents became a focus due to the consultation carried out with parents/carers. Many felt unsure about how they could support their children's learning and seemed reluctant to contribute to their children's Learning Journeys. As a result of this the buddy group attended specifically designed training around working with parents.

During these sessions the group decided to design and deliver a programme of workshops aimed at building relationships between Key Persons and parents/carers through supporting children's learning. The eight weekly sessions are practical and informative, and build on what parents do at home with their children – going shopping, cooking, bath time, etc. Resources bags include equipment and materials to support the activities, disposable cameras and observation slips to encourage parents/carers to 'look, listen and note'.

Further to this all foundation stage practitioners are now involved in parents' meetings and transition meetings for their key group children.

Buddying with early years settings in our locality has enabled us to support many children through the often-difficult transition to school. Key Persons have visited the day nursery to do story times or to visit children who will be moving to our school. Practitioners from the day nursery have also attended gradual admission visits in to school.

Practitioners from both school and setting also attend the 'Parents as Partners' workshops to further build relationships and share ideas and practice.

What are the responsibilities of the Key Person?

- to support transitions;
- to compile Learning Journeys;
- to deliver planned group times;
- to plan and deliver Key Person time (based on children's interests, and incorporating Social and Emotional Aspects of Development (SEAD)/Social and Emotional Aspects of Learning (SEAL) activities);
- to talk to parents on a daily basis and at formal parents meetings.

Do you provide any key group times throughout the day or week?

- meeting and greeting and end of the day;
- snack time;
- lunchtime – each key group has a consistent lunchtime officer; practitioners also eat with children wherever possible, particularly during transition times;
- one focused key group time in nursery;
- a minimum of three key group times, each week, in reception.

What training has been accessed to support the role?

- attachment and the role of the Key Person;
- parents as partners: working together to support children's learning;
- SEAD and SEAL training.

What impact have the changes had on children, families, staff and school?

Children appear happier and have developed strong bonds with their Key Person, often seeking them out for comfort or praise. Building strong relationships with parents and welcoming them into the classrooms seems to have developed a stronger sense of belonging for many children.

Families and parents are more confident now they have a 'named' person to talk to about their child. Many children have older siblings who were in nursery; we are able to continue building on these relationships with families. Parents are more confident that someone is looking out for their child and taking the time to get to know them well.

Teaching assistants have been given more responsibility and opportunity to build strong attachments with a small group of children. Practitioners now feel more valued by children, parents and other staff.

Our next development is going to be to introduce the Key Person role into Year 1.

TABLE 5.4 Process of the project

TIME	TASK	HOW	WHO
Phase 1	■ Explore the role of the Key Person ■ Explore the ideology of 'Intimacy Island'	■ Staff meeting ■ Staff discussion ■ Exploring text i.e. 'attachment theory', 'people under 3'	■ Whole staff team ■ Birth to 3 practice development officer ■ Children's centre teacher
Phase 2	■ Research into and reflection on current practice ■ Identify implications for the setting and suggest ways forward	■ Video record practice before, during and after lunchtime ■ View footage, discuss positive practice and identify areas for development	■ Manager ■ Room leaders ■ Centre workers ■ Support workers ■ Birth to 3 practice development officer ■ Children's centre teacher
Phase 3	■ Implement Intimacy Island ■ Developing ideas of activity for Intimacy Island	■ Agree ways forward ■ Develop action plan ■ Staff meeting to discuss and share ideas of activities for Intimacy Island	■ Manager ■ Room leaders ■ Centre workers ■ Birth to Three Practice Development Officer ■ Children's Centre Teacher
Phase 4	■ Assess the impact on the outcomes for children ■ Working with parents	■ Child observations and learning stories ■ Video record practice ■ Review video and identify developments ■ Celebrate achievements	■ Whole staff team ■ Birth to 3 practice development officer ■ Children's centre teacher
Phase 5 ongoing	■ Monitoring practice, addressing challenges and dilemmas ■ Maintain the quality of Intimacy Island on a daily basis	■ Regularly discuss and reflect ■ Keep as a set item on team meeting agenda ■ Observe daily practice	■ Manager ■ Room leaders ■ Centre workers ■ Children's centre teacher

Example 6: Implementing the Key Kersons approach (Anna Fitzpatrick, Advisory Teacher Oxfordshire County Council)

This is the story of one small day nursery where training and support from an advisory teacher has had an impact on establishing and giving confidence to managers to get started. Two practitioners, one working with children under 2 and one working with 3- to 4-year-olds, came on Key Person training. Engaging in the training made them realise they could not implement the Key Persons approach on their own; they would have to get the owner of the nursery on board. With the encouragement of their advisory teacher, the owner attended the training, her first course in many years, which she said she enjoyed very much. As a result, the Key Persons approach was introduced more systematically, into the Nursery. Each Key Person informed parents about this individually and the responsibilities were explained. Most parents seemed to know about the fact that their child would be entitled to a Key Person. Some would ask about who would be their child's Key Person.

How the approach works at present in the nursery

- Key Persons are assigned groups of children with buddies to support when staff are on holiday, off sick, etc.

- The Key Person/buddy greets the child and family in the morning and says farewell when the family leave. This is really noticeable as when parents/carers come, the staff nearest to the door let the Key Person know one of the parents from their group has arrived. The Key Person then takes time for an informal exchange of information. In the past the parents only had a chance to talk with the person who welcomed them at the door.

- When a child starts at the nursery the Key Person meets with the parents/carers and gathers information about the child including details of the immediate and the wider family and any languages they speak, customs or traditions they have.

- They attend to children's personal care, and the younger children are fed by their Key Person.

- The Key People in the older children's room have their special times at snack-time and lunchtime, making them informal, relaxed and social occasions.

- The Key Person has responsibility for making observations of their children's learning and for planning for individual needs.

- The Key People have also just started a system of tracking children's development, to monitor whether they are providing the range of experiences that the children are entitled to.

- In the autumn the staff made links with two of the schools the children were going to attend, to ensure smooth transitions and found it very beneficial sharing information about the children with the next Key Person.

- New staff are not assigned key children at first. Their induction involves having the role of the Key Person discussed and modelled by the established Key People and nearly all are sent on the training.

The manager has said that the Key Persons approach ensures that their practice is much more personal for the children and families, rather than a haphazard way of meeting their needs. The other noticeable development is the attitude of the owner. The training and the consequent implementation of the approach has made a difference, so that each child who attends the nursery has become special. One child whom she had concerns about, who had moved onto school, was still in her mind a term later and she was happy when she discovered he had settled in well.

Next steps

The manager plans:

- to give out a questionnaire to parents on how they feel about the Key Persons approach;
- to create a Key Person information sheet for parents, explaining the role in much more depth;
- to evaluate the way the Key Persons approach is working in the nursery.

Example 7: An account of the the Key Persons approach in practice (Wendy Baker, Nursery Teacher in a primary school)

I first became a Key Person at a nursery school in a children's centre four years ago. It was a completely new experience for me and, as a nursery nurse, involved a great deal more responsibility than I had ever had before. It was the beginning of an understanding of the importance of attachment and how it affects children's learning and development.

My experience began with home visits for the children who would form part of my key group. This meant that even before the child or parent had started, or maybe even visited the setting, they had a familiar face to connect with. This was the basis of a bond and a building of trust that would last for … well, is it ever truly forgotten?

During my time at this setting I had a group of children each with their particular needs and interests, including some with very specialised needs. Without doubt, the bond formed with these children enabled them to access and experience a range of opportunities available to them, with the confidence that someone was close by to support them when required. I also observed how children coped when their Key Person was absent as they formed relationships with other staff. Families spoke of how they appreciated having one particular person with whom to liaise. This relationship also played a huge part in assisting children transitioning to reception classes.

Several years on I have now become a nursery teacher in a primary school.

Key Persons approach: what's that?

Moving to a primary school where early years is a small cog in a big wheel was rather a culture shock. Priorities were completely different, predictably with concerns regarding children's behaviour and their attainment. However, by using my prior knowledge and experience I do feel confident in introducing the importance of positive attachments and the benefits they offer to both staff and families. One term in and I'm beginning to implement key group time as a way of starting each day, immediately reducing the frantic beginning of each day when children were looking for support as parents were leaving.

Of course, all experiences can be learned from and the two very different, contrasting experiences have raised questions in my own practice which are worth considering.

For example, how much responsibility should support staff have and how should confidential issues be shared between the class teacher and the Key Person, as it is the teacher with the ultimate responsibility for the class? Ultimately, I believe it is important to make the Key Persons approach work for you, your setting and, most importantly, the children and their families. It is an approach that is individual to each situation and systems or routines may need to be adjusted to find what is right for you. It really is worth taking time and effort to get it right.

Theme B: The importance of continuity of a Key Person through the early years setting and into Key Stage 1

Example 8: Managing transitions (Jo Vickers, Head, Weavers Field Community Nursery, Tower Hamlets)

As manager of a new nursery I became concerned that the babies and baby room staff were confined to a very small space. The baby room was registered by Ofsted for six babies. Although this is an ideal size for developing relationships and being able to care for babies in a small intimate environment, it became apparent that the room was less than ideal for babies as they began to crawl and toddle, and they needed more space to move around. In addition, the babies did not have any direct access to the nursery garden.

On speaking to the staff team it also became apparent that the baby room staff felt isolated from the rest of the activities of the nursery. They were also concerned that several of the children in the main room had a Key Person who was spending most of their time in the baby room. There were times during the day when they needed their Key Person. The dilemma the nursery faced was whether children needed to change their Key Person or whether to develop a mixed age/family grouped nursery?

The nursery was obviously not meeting the needs of all of the children. In addition, there were times when the baby room was over-staffed, and the main room staff were struggling to cover all of the activities expected of them.

The idea of changing Key Persons went against the ethos of the nursery. All staff agreed that if children changed their Key Person, it would not stop them wanting to see them. It was decided that a mixed age group was a possibility, if the team worked together to enable the change.

The change became a positive experience for all of the children, in the nursery. Most importantly, children now keep the same Key Person throughout their time in nursery.

Stephen started the nursery at 11 months. The manager recognised prior to Stephen starting nursery that it was going to be a difficult separation for both Stephen and his mother. A long settling-in period was agreed between the nursery and parents. This proved to be particularly invaluable. Stephen did take a couple of months to settle into the nursery. Stephen's mother got to know the staff and particularly Stephen's Key Person extremely well, and although Stephen was unsettled for a few months Stephen's mother said she always felt complete trust in the nursery, and that this had enabled her to go back to work, knowing that Stephen was well looked after. Stephen's mother and father both wanted Stephen to have consistent care. They were concerned about his emotional well-being and were very keen to ensure Stephen experienced a minimum of transitions during the first five years. Stephen was able to have same Key Person throughout his time in nursery. Stephen has recently left the nursery to enter reception. His transition to reception has been smooth, and his father remarked that the trust Stephen had in his Key Person had enabled her to help Stephen understand what it would be like at school. His father said, 'Stephen just knew what would happen, and had accepted that he might feel sad at first, but it would get better.'

The nursery is small and staff and children get to know each other very well. Stephen became very confident in nursery. The initial transition from home to nursery was gradual, sensitive and provided time for relationships to develop. Children continue to need their Key Person as they get older,; even as they develop new friendships and relationships with other adults. This Key Person relationship proved to be invaluable to Stephen throughout his time in nursery and in supporting his transition to school.

Example 9: A parent's perspective on the stresses of transitions without Key Person support (sent by Teresa Asquith, Advisory Teacher, Haringey)

The nursery was such a big space and I was worried about how O would cope without me. She had a Key Person and that helped. I could go to this Key Person and tell her very personal things about O and she would listen and I was aware that she shared this with the other staff which made me feel that O was safe whoever she was with. O knew she could go to her Key Person whenever she needed something. She had a co-Key Person whenever her Key Person was away. I really did feel that her Key Person knew her best.

Eventually O became especially close to her Key Person, very fond of her. She talked about her at home in a very positive way: 'She said I was lovely', she would say, especially if she was being naughty at home! It was like she used her as someone to stick up for her even when she wasn't there! If her Key Person was away then O would look at me to check that I thought the co-Key Person was going to be alright. O had one Key Person all the way through her two years in nursery.

Transfer to reception was difficult. To begin with the teacher didn't come in to meet the children before she started at the school and O and I worried all summer about what she would be like. I didn't know who her Key Person was or even if she had one. When a friend told me she would have one I asked the school, and found out that, yes, she did have one. I then asked her if she knew all about O's history and she said no, she hadn't read any notes yet. I was upset about this. I felt she should know about my child in order to support her. O definitely didn't know she had a Key Person until I told her. All the staff seemed very nice but I didn't know who to go to if O was upset after a contact visit. O was not happy to leave the nursery – she kept saying, 'I can see it (nursery) but do you know I am not allowed to go in there?'

O lost confidence and didn't want to be left in the reception class, even though they did phase the children in gradually. I accept that change is probably more difficult for O than for others, but then she could have had more support.

Theme C: The impact of the Key Persons approach

Example 10: Noticing the effect of loss of security when a child attends another nursery during the holiday period (Jo Vickers, Head, Weavers Field Community Nursery, Tower Hamlets)

During inset training on emotional well-being, Key People were asked to think about and discuss a child who they felt 'was doing well' in the nursery. All of the Key People suggested one child. The majority of staff picked one of their key children.

E is 14 months old. His Key Person described why she thought E was doing well; she described E as always being happy, never getting upset. He enjoyed exploring the nursery, following all of the older children around, sleeping well and really enjoying his food. She also added that 'he just enjoyed being with the other children and got on well with all of the adults in the nursery'. All of the adults nodded and agreed that E was doing well. Staff also added that he was a robust little boy and enjoyed the company of the older boys in particular. On returning from the Christmas break, E wasn't his usual self. His Key Person remarked, 'So much for thinking E's emotional well-being was high.' E came into nursery crying today. This was something E had never done in the past. It was suggested that maybe the break had unsettled him and his routines had probably been different. During that day and the following days, E seemed to settle but it was noticeable that he was seeking out his Key Person more than normal and seemed particularly clingy when she held another child. This was very much out of character for E, who had always been happy to share his Key Person.

On speaking to E's father at collection time a few days later, E's father remarked that E was very happy to be back at the nursery and that although the nursery E had attended during the Christmas break was 'alright', E preferred this nursery. His father said he had noticed how happy E was to be back at nursery.

I was taken aback by these comments. Further enquiries revealed that E's mother's employers had provided details of a nursery providing emergency cover for children whose main nurseries were closed during the holiday break. Key People were upset by this news and felt that there was a misunderstanding by some parents, that when a child had settled into nursery and had a good relationship with their Key Person they would be happy anywhere. I discussed this with the staff team, and it was suggested that there was a need to support parents to have a better understanding about transitions.

Example 11: The impact of being attached to a child; remembering and cherishing attachments with key children who have moved on; finding a way to 'let go' at the end of the relationship for Key Persons and children (Hazel Harris, Eastwood Nursery Centre)

About three years ago I had a little 3-year-old girl called Lauren in my key group. She immediately bonded with me although she was a bit anxious to begin with. At first she didn't like her mum to leave so I made sure that she was always part of the key group and involved her as much as possible. If I couldn't give her my attention then I would give her something I thought she would like, which was usually my necklace. This was because each morning when she came in she would immediately look to see if I was wearing a necklace and then she would comment on it.

Two years ago I bumped into Lauren about a year after she had left nursery and the first thing she said to me was, 'Hazel, I like your necklace.' This brought back to me the relationship that we had together. In a moment of weakness I gave her the necklace I was wearing which she immediately put on. As we said goodbye her mum said, 'Hazel, she won't take that off now.'

At the weekend I was in a local restaurant with my family. Lauren, who was with her family, saw me and immediately came over and gave me a kiss and a cuddle. Later in the afternoon as she left the restaurant she handed me a little note – 'I love you', written on the edge of a paper napkin.

Example 12: The impact of the Key Persons approach for a 3-year-old and his mother (Tina Jones, Eastwood Nursery Centre)

Mark was 3 years old when he came to the nursery. Our customary home visit revealed a very anxious mother who was very concerned about her son starting nursery. She was anxious because he had a fascination with locks and she described him as a 'Little Houdini'. She said there were no environments that he couldn't get out of. She also said that he would, and could, climb anything, open any door or lock. She described him as 'hyperactive', a child who was always on the go and looking for attention. She was very worried that he would get out of the classrooms and the building without anyone knowing. In spite of the high fences that surrounded the nursery garden Mark's mum feared that he would climb over them and escape and nobody would know.

The reason I believe the Key Persons approach worked so well for Mark was because his mum knew that he had someone special keeping an eye on him. She was happy that she could physically hand him over to the same person each morning. Mark also benefited from knowing who he was being handed to in the morning. If his Key Person wasn't in he would cling to mum, not wanting to go into the room or play with any activities. When he saw his Key Person his face would light up and he would take her hand and happily access the activities that were set up around the classroom. Mum became more relaxed knowing that she had the Key Person to share information with; she found it more personal. It took a while for mum to trust and feel able to disclose what life was like at home with four children. She had three boys and one girl. All the boys appeared to have a special need. His mum found it hard to discuss her personal life so I think it worked well for the family knowing that they had one person to deal with. Even though we had the buddy system Mark's mum found it much easier to go directly to the Key Person. Mark became more settled over the year. We built on his personal interests. We worked hard to provide a consistent environment with clear boundaries and expectations, which enabled him to access the broader curriculum. Mark has since moved out of the borough but he and his mum still come to visit.

Example 13: The impact of the Key Person's role on an anxious child (Sarah-Jane Samuels, Eastwood Nursery Centre)

Avril was at Eastwood for two years. When she first started nursery she was a quiet, reserved child. She was referred to Eastwood by the speech and language team (SLT) because she was a reluctant talker. I worked very closely with the SLT on an agreed programme. Initially the SLT worked with her mum in the setting. I was then introduced to the group. I worked closely with mum, the SLT and Avril. Avril would talk in front of mum in a familiar environment. Gradually we worked together and built up a relationship and slowly she grew more confident talking to me in front of mum. These sessions went on for nearly a year before she started talking to me in the classroom. During key group time I encouraged Avril to hold familiar objects to give her the support and confidence she needed to help her speak. She was never put under any pressure to speak. After about a year and a half she began to speak in our key group sessions. Mum and dad were also invited to join our key group time. Her parents were very supportive of the Key Persons approach and I feel this was instrumental in giving Avril the confidence she needed to speak in her key group. Avril went from strength to strength and became a very communicative little girl within the nursery. With the birth of her baby sister Avril lost a bit of her confidence but this was soon regained with the help of forward planning with the parents on how best to manage the arrival of the new baby. Before the baby was born I met with Avril's mum and talked about some of the things I could do in key group time relating to babies and some of things that they could do at home. The sessions at nursery were very successful and I was able to draw on the experiences of other children in the group who had recently had babies in their family. The topic of babies carried on after Avril's sister was born. Avril's mum first brought the baby in to show her to Avril's friends and later brought her to give her a bath.

At the end of the school year I met with Avril's parents to discuss how best to manage her transition from nursery to school. Together we devised a simple plan in line with the nursery's policy on transition. I invited Avril's new teacher to observe Avril in the nursery. This observation was crucial in establishing Avril's ability. I accompanied Avril and her to visit her new school. We took photos and later made a book about her new school, which she took home to share with her family. After starting her new school, Avril's mother phoned me to inform me that Avril had settled in well. We are still in touch with the family and are expecting to have her younger sister at nursery soon.

Example 14: The dilemmas and challenges in relation to the loss of a child (Jackie Dolan, Manager, Children's Centre)

How do we support staff (and parents) with the emotional demands of the Key Persons approach in relation to the loss of a child? This centre has a Special Care Unit where children with complex health needs are placed; these children often have life-limiting conditions (two children have died this year so far). It is part of the wider centre, so we still work within the guidelines of the EYFS. It is a very complex issue, as to how the staff are supported but also how are we equipped to support the parents after such a loss as well as continue to act professionally and contain the other children and families. Often parents come back to us to share the life of the child (just recently a parent came in to celebrate the birthday of her child who had passed away in February).

With inclusion as one of the key drivers in early years provision today, many practitioners are now working with children who have complex health needs, often with life-limiting conditions. Children who need intimate personal care to a degree that is far more 'intimate and complex' are in need of real attunement with practitioners. As with all children (and their families), there are many emotional aspects to the role as Key Person. However, I believe there is a deeper level of trust required between parents and the Key Person when their child is totally dependent and has a limited life expectancy.

Recently (and sadly not the first time), one of the children who attended the centre died quite suddenly at home, the second loss in the year. As a manager I was sad for the parents, and then my thoughts shifted to the Key Person and team. It was my first experience of having to support a team of people with such a loss. It raised lots of questions for me, as to how they had previously been supported through this significant event and how I would now support them. What would the support look like? How do we support the parents? Are we expected to support the parents? What about the rest of the team? How do we remember the child? How do we carry on with the 'day job'?

I had been informed by the team in the past they simply 'had been left to get on with it'; for me this was not an option. On one occasion a staff member was informed of a child's death while she was 'bending down placing another child in a standing frame'. I was sure I needed to do something to enable the team to reflect and feel contained. I was just not clear as to how I should proceed.

I have met with the team since the loss and we have listened to each other about the feelings it raises for each of us. Being well aware of the emotional demands the KPA requires already, this final separation is completely unique and brings with it many new dilemmas, and evokes worries and feelings in individuals, including me. As the manager I recognise I am not qualified or equipped to follow this type of work through completely with the team. I have since arranged some counselling, for the team and individually if they so wish.

On discussion with the team we thought about some key things that need some consideration for us as a centre and certainly for me as a manager. These have included:

- How are staff told of the loss, by whom and when?
- What happens if the Key Person/team member/manager is not in the centre? Do we call them at home to prepare them before they come back?
- How do we tell the other children?
- How do we tell the other parents (especially those whose children are equally poorly)?
- Is it appropriate to attend a service/funeral? Who should attend?
- Is it appropriate to become upset? How upset?
- What about the feelings of stress we feel when we have to tell other parents?
- How should we remember the children – what is appropriate?
- How does the centre acknowledge/mark the loss – bearing in mind it is a 'happy' place for children and families?
- Supporting parents after a death who come back to celebrate their child's life – how do we do this? Is it our job?
- How are we expected to contain the children and families we work with, with such 'heavy hearts'.
- How do we handle feelings of guilt/embarrassment which have come from allowing ourselves to feel hurt and upset? What must the parents be feeling?
- How do we receive 'permission' to be sad?
- How do we cope knowing other children may be close to the end of their lives?
- Going home after a day's work, what do we tell our families?

These issues were raised in a short discussion with the immediate team. Since then staff have accessed some professional counselling and continue to act as Key People to the rest of the group. Having the discussion has brought to the surface personal feelings and events (losses) in individuals lives and, with that, feelings of guilt in allowing those to come through when we are 'supposed to be thinking of the child'.

Example 15: The impact of the Key Person in supporting attachments at home (anonymous)

V first came to us when she was approximately 14 months old. She was living in the care of her mother who told us that she did not get on with her own mother who was very controlling. She did not have any contact with her and under no circumstances were we to have any communication with her. This of course we respected.

V settled in well in our under-2 room and built a very good relationship with her Key Person. At the beginning, mum was very chatty, talking to the Key Person about her (very ambitious) plans for the future and we were beginning to discuss her need for adult company and how we could help with this (she was not interested in Stay and Play groups).

One day we had a phone call from V's grandmother to tell us that mum had been taken into hospital and sectioned, and therefore she was now looking after V. We could not, of course, just accept this story so contacted social services to verify the truth. Once all was confirmed we then focused on the impact of this sudden change for V. Her mother had 'disappeared' and she was now being cared for by someone that she had not had any contact with for over a year, so was a stranger as far as she was concerned. The Key Person and I met with the grandmother to discuss the support we could offer. She was in a position to be able to pay for nursery fees and in fact decided that it would be very helpful to increase the amount of time that she attended. We all thought this was very positive as the Key Person was the one stable relationship in V's life.

As staff, we were also conscious of the impact that the situation was having on grandmother's life. She was very committed to helping her daughter and grand-daughter, but was having to attend meetings with the hospital, social services, etc. almost on a daily basis. She had recently retired, had taken up golf and joined a couple of other classes but had to stop these because she had no time for them any longer. As well as coping with the practical issues this created, she was also having to come to terms with a huge change in her expectations for her retirement. The Key Person was again someone who she was seeing frequently and who was able to give time to listen to her.

V then reached her second birthday. We would have considered keeping her in the under-2 room but thought she needed the stimulation of being with her peers, and we had a new child booked to take up her place. The implication of this was that she would have a new Key Person from the over-3s room. It was purely by chance that another staff member from the over-3s room left at that time and so we moved V's Key Person into that room. It was fortunate that she had no preference which room she worked in. We also thought it would not have a massive impact on her other key children as they were all in stable home situations and therefore continuity for V should take priority.

Very gradually the mother's health is improving and she is now living at home with grandmother and her daughter. This means, however, that V has to accept and build a renewed relationship with her mother – someone who has 'let her down' by suddenly 'disappearing' from her day-to-day life. Again the relationship with the Key Person is vitally important.

Theme D: Maintaining the Key Persons approach when it is established

Example 16: Building, maintaining and developing the Key Persons approach in two children's centres (Ann Thurgood, Manager, First Steps in Bath)

I work for a voluntary organisation which runs two children's centres on behalf of Bath and North East Somerset County Council. The day care in the centre has places for 60 children. Our registration is from birth until school age; however, we only take babies under 6 months in extreme situations of need. They are cared for in two rooms – one for children under 2 years and the second for those over age 2. We feel it is important to allow as much flexibility as possible regarding the children's hours of attendance in order to meet the needs of the families. They can therefore book their children in for half-hour slots throughout the day. The result is that we have children arriving and leaving throughout the day, and last year had approximately 144 children attending at some point during each week.

Ensuring that all children and their families are well supported is therefore challenging. There are about 15 staff, some of whom work part time, and this means that each full-time staff member can act as Key Person for about 15 children. The Key Persons approach has been used almost since the original nursery first started so it is well embedded into our practice. We feel it is the only way in which we could possibly relate to all these children and families effectively.

Inducting new staff into the Key Persons approach

When a new member of staff starts, they are given a careful induction during their three month probationary period. We have developed a checklist of the various policies, procedures, etc. that they need not just to come know, but also to absorb into their thinking and approach. This of course includes an induction into the Key Persons approach and what that means for us. We have a written description of the Key Person role and how it is implemented in our setting, and this is discussed by the new person and the line manager. All staff have monthly supervision meetings with their line manager, but during the three-month induction programme this takes place more frequently. A normal pattern for this is to meet daily for the first two or three days, then weekly and then decreasing to monthly, but it is very flexible according to the experience of the person and how they develop. The amount of support needed is very varied so the induction programme needs to be carefully tailored to each individual. We consider that, although this costs a considerable amount in managerial time, it is time well invested. This cannot be rushed. In the long term it is a good investment as they are likely to become much more effective, more satisfied and more committed to their role.

We also assign a mentor to the new staff member. This is, whenever possible, a colleague at the same grade. The purpose of this is so that they can ask a colleague/friend questions that they may not feel comfortable to ask their line manager. The mentor also works alongside the new person regarding the Key Person role. The mentor models the interaction with the children and with the family, introducing the new person to the children and families who will become their responsibility. They work together to observe the children and to build their Learning Journals, ensure they are fully informed about the family background and together plan appropriate activities for the children. It is only after the three months probation that they formally take on the role. Again we feel this should not be rushed as they need to fully understand the way in which we interpret the role and we need to be sure they have the necessary skills. We find that qualified staff have usually focused on relating to children during their training, but not all have considered the particular skills required when relating to their families. We aim to enable staff to approach families not so much as partners with us but as partners with them in that that we are offering a resource that is available to them to enable them to raise their children. It is too easy to inadvertently come across to families as judgemental, as 'experts' or as someone with the solution, none of which build their esteem as parents/carers.

Working with parents

We have a parents' handbook, which we give to them during the registration process. This is written in a 'frequently asked questions' format, which was chosen as we thought it would be less likely to come across to parents as 'instructions to follow'. The information about the Key Person role reads as follows:

> Your child will be given a Key Person who will be your usual first point of contact on a daily basis. The Key Person is responsible for the welfare of your child and keeps a learning diary of what your child can do, in order to help them reach their full potential. These diaries contain photographs of your child at play, pictures they have created, observations from your child's Key Person and the other staff and quotes from your child. Throughout the year you will be invited to reviews with your Key Person when you will be able to discuss your child's progress and what they may work on next.

The manager or assistant manager meet with a new family and together they complete the registration form, which focuses on business matters. The child then attends, with the family, for two settling in sessions. During these visits the Key Person spends time with the child and gives a 'welcome' letter to their new families that introduces themselves and briefly explains the role. They also complete 'settling in forms' with the family so they can discover the child's likes and dislikes, health needs, etc. It is a very important opportunity for the Key Person to start to get to know both child and family.

Managing individual work with children whilst keeping a 'team ethos'

The major challenge relates to the difficulty of sharing information across all staff who 'need to know'. This requires very good teamwork, which is hard in a busy room but would be even harder if we did not have Key People. The rooms are overseen by senior practitioners and so they know a great deal about all the children and their families. We have a 'family update file'. This is held in a secure cupboard and has a sheet for each family. Any information that is important for all staff to know is written in there by the Key Person. It is the responsibility of staff to check this file regularly to ensure they have the latest knowledge. There is also a staff message book where the Key Person can tell other staff when there is new information to read about a particular family.

When the Key Person knows in advance that they will be away, they inform the parents and let them know which other member of staff will be especially looking after their child in the Key Person's place, and introduce them whenever possible. If the Key Person is away without notice, the senior practitioners explain to the parents on arrival, and reassures them that, as we work as a close team, we all know the children well anyway (and the children know us).

First Steps senior management team (that is the director and four team managers) meets weekly to discuss general matters. We take time at this meeting once a month to share updates and to reflect on the support being offered to our most vulnerable children and families. One of our other challenges is in raising staff awareness of services available to families. We work with a great many other agencies and it is hard to make sure all staff know what services they can suggest in different situations. We used one of our recent training days to help with this. We invited our partners to join us and to talk for a few minutes each to explain their role. This solved the issue for current staff but we now have to ensure new staff have the information and that staff are kept up to date – especially as expected changes impact on us.

Example 17: Working together as a group: one aspect of the Key Person's journey in early years settings; an example of reflective practitioners thinking about a child together (Dorothy Y. Selleck, Early Years Consultant)

This example documents conversations between early years practitioners with their mentor. The conversation focused on a child and his family so as to give support to the Key Person struggling to build an attachment relationship with a new child in her group. These are the actual words of the people in the group as remembered and recorded in the mentor's notes but the names and some details have been changed to protect the children and adults in this account. This discussion combines episodes from Key Person conversations in early years settings and schools so as to explore the challenge and complexity of developing relationships in families similar to our own as well as different from our own.

Utkrushta is 4 years old and Tanya is his Key Person. He has been attending the nursery for two months. Joan is paired with Tanya for their Key Person work together. Annabel is a family worker and works with parent groups. Dorcas is a mentor supporting the team to develop their Key Persons approach.

Tanya   *I am worried about Utkrushta and finding it difficult to bond with him as he doesn't speak any English yet. He destroys everything, he bites the dolls and he finds it hard to join in, even in the Key Person group times. It is so hard when I am trying to build a bond with him and the others – I wonder if our key group times are too big?*

Dorcas   *What language does he speak at home?*

Tanya   *Not sure … some sort of Asain – or is it Arabic?*

Joan   *I think Utkrushta speaks Urdu. We are Key Person buddies and at the moment we have key group time with our two groups together. This allows one of us to give individual support for Utkrushta and for Ruby too – she has cochlear implants and also needs help to be included in key group time. But that means we have 10 or more in the group – it is not really working as the group is too big for intimacy and informality.*

Dorcas   *Why do you think Utkrushta breaks and destroys things?*

Tanya   [pause for thought] *I think it is really frustrating for him … we try to spend time with him on his own but it is difficult. He gets really hard to manage when he does not understand and cannot tell us what he wants. The other day he just stamped on my foot.* [she grimaces] *It really hurt!! It is so hard when I cannot communicate in his language.*

Dorcas   *You seem to be communicating very dramatically and effectively even without words! He was able to express his frustration when he wanted to protest to you – his Key Person – very forcibly. You looked really hurt and upset as you told me. I wonder if Utkrushta also needed to see that you were hurt – to be sure you had listened to how he was feeling? Did he understand that you were hurt or cross? I expect yelping 'OUCH' can be understood in any language?*

Joan   *That's right he does do that to get attention – so in a way you are communicating with him even though it feels so hard when neither of you have words in each other's language.*

Dorcas   *Have you thought that it is because he is developing a bond with you that he is using aggressive protest as a way of connecting with you so as to test you, to call for your involvement in his play or perhaps to project on to you the pain he is experiencing of feeling left out or misunderstood? Can you bear to think about his stamping on your foot as his first steps in building up a special relationship with you?* [Tanya is thoughtful, looks doubtful and glances towards her buddy.]

Joan   *Yes, Tanya works really hard with Utkrushta, I think you (Tanya) don't realise how much he is settling! Remember how it took ages with Usman last year but gradually we built up a relationship with him with the help of the family workers. Annabel ran that group for the dads and they came and took photos of the children in the nursery. Also the parents met upstairs, they did that map in the family room with all the pins to show where everybody was from. After that it was easier to get the involvement of the parents in here too. Then parents seemed more at ease in the nursery and did not rush off. Some of them even joined in key group time for a little while at the beginning of the day.*

Tanya   *I was thinking of that time with Usman – it was so weird. Do you remember at home time when he knelt and touched my feet. I thought at last he is playing with me – a kind of game – we were friends at last! So I joined in and touched his feet too and laughed with him. But Usman recoiled and looked horrified, embarrassed even. Luckily one of the other Asian mothers in my key group saw it happen. I know her really well and she soon put me right!! She said that in her family that was a way of saying goodbye to adults. A sign of affection and respect for aunties and that is why Usman had touched my feet and why he was confused when I did it back. Thank goodness I had built the relationship over time so that she could explain to me – we did laugh! It is so easy to get these cultural things wrong and upset someone.*

Joan   *So … it is early days yet with Utkrushta. You are really experienced with these children – what would you like me to do tomorrow so that you can have a bit of bonding time with him on his own?*

What do you think? Something like this or something else?

- If you had been a part of this discussion what would you have felt and thought?

- What would this discussion help you to think about in your own relationships with the key children in your group?

- Have you had similar experiences or misunderstandings with families from cultures different to your own?

- What might you have said next to support Tanya with developing an attachment with Utkrushta and his family?

- Do you think the key group was too big?

- What could you say about the relationship between the paired Key Persons, Tanya and Joan?

- What did they achieve in this session as they reflected on Tanya's Key Person work with Utkrushta?

- What more do Tanya and Joan need to know about Utkrushta and his family to help them with learning English as a second language?

- If you were Tanya's manager what would you do?

- If you were Tanya's partner at home what would you say if she came home upset and told you about Utkrushta?

- If you were the family worker how would you help Tanya nurture her relationship with Utkrushta and his parents?

- What have you learnt from this episode to help you with your own work with your key children?

Example 18: The Key Persons approach with 3 to 5s – a practitioner's perspective – issues, difficulties and possibilities (Lesley Ferguson, Nursery Teacher)

The Key Persons approach in practice

I was a young class teacher in the late 1980s and early 1990s teaching reception and year one classes of 30-plus children on my own, with occasional support from a teaching assistant or a volunteer. The idea that a teacher would have the opportunity to focus her attention on a much smaller group of children seemed like a luxury and beyond the realms of possibility.

More recently I have worked in a range of early years settings, all of which have used a Key Persons approach. In these settings, and especially in large nurseries with 40, 50, 60 or more children per session, the Key Persons approach fosters attachments between key members of staff and individual and small groups of children.

Without a Key Persons approach it is very difficult for staff to form meaningful relationships with many of the children. It is my view that this is essential for the successful learning and development of all children and especially for the quieter, more timid ones who may become lost in a large nursery environment and often struggle to cope.

Based on a range of experiences from a number of different nursery settings I want to explore some of the issues I have faced or observed related to implementing the Key Persons approach in practice alongside possible ways it might be strengthened or developed.

Setting the scene

Children at settings I have worked in recently are being admitted younger now than in recent years. They may be coming into very large nursery environments and some find it a very big step to take. It is the first time they have ever been away from home on a regular basis. They often take a long time to settle and having a Key Person to build a relationship with from the start is vital to the success of their settling and to making the painful separation from home and from their main or only attachment figure. Often children have not been to playgroups, pre-schools or parent/toddler groups whereas a small number have been in under 3s units so are very familiar with the 'away from home' environment.

The nurseries have had a range of strategies in place to make the transition as easy as possible for the children. Some close the nursery for a few days at the beginning of the school year to visit every new child in her or his home. At the start of the term there are open days where children can visit the setting with their parents or family.

Children are divided into groups with one Key Person per group. This gives each child and her/his family a Key Person who will get to know them very well. Wherever possible the Key Person is the adult who home visits them and becomes someone the child can go to if they need support, comfort or attention. It is also someone to share excitements with, to read them a story, and is the person who will get to know each child's needs, interests and development the best.

Generally in the settings, all adults have worked with all the children during the main part of each session, in both indoor and outdoor environments. At the end of each session the children meet with their own group and their individual Key Person. There they have had the opportunity to get to know the Key Person and the other children in the group well and begin to develop a sense of identity as a member of their group. Some of the settings have had this group time in the middle of the session.

Many factors have arisen when matching children to Key People. It is not always possible to keep the same Key Person with all the children the Key Person has visited at home, although mostly the settings would have tried to.

Some of the settings have felt it is important to find out if children's older siblings attended the nursery. In order to maintain continuity with the same families, they would try to match each child with the same Key Person as their sibling. Younger children may already know the Key Person and the Key Person already knows about the family, their needs and interests and so on.

Organising all of this has huge implications for administration. Arranging home visits for over 100 children is an extremely tall order. In some settings the administration staff manages this. Other settings have left it to the Key People who have had little time. Ideally it should be worked out between administration staff and the Key Persons who are more likely to know the children and families already. It would probably require more days allocated to home visiting (meaning nursery closures), more home visits made by the Key People and more non-contact time given to the Key People. Co-Key Persons and bilingual staff should accompany the main Key

Person wherever possible. Even if families are known, there may still be issues of group dynamics, special educational needs, English as an additional language, gender balance, etc. that cannot always be known in advance and changes will be needed. It is a complex and time-consuming process.

Where parents requests a particular Key Person for various reasons, staff have as far as possible been assigned to undertake that home visit. The administration staff may not have remembered or recognised from a new application that this was a family previously known to the setting. Sometimes siblings have different surnames.

Children can be swapped at a later stage to the group whose Key Person knows the family. Other reasons have occurred, too, for changing the Key Person from the one who home-visited. It may have been that the balance for a group would be difficult, for example that there have been too many children with behaviour or other significant difficulties, or an imbalance of gender or ethnicity. My experience of the ideal situation though is when the Key Person is there right at the beginning and has seen the children in their home environments.

It seems crucial to me that the home visit is, wherever possible, the beginning of a relationship between the Key Person and the family that continues right through their time at nursery until they leave.

Some suggestions for strengthening Key Persons practice

From under 3 to over 3: a loss of continuity?

In each of the settings of my experience, when children progress from under-3s units to 3 to 5 nursery, there has been a change of Key Person. This has meant that the security and continuity of the relationship and of progression is lost or diminished. In settings where there is a lack of contact with the next stage Key Person, staff could be enabled to move with their key children to address the continuity issues. However, this would be more difficult when the children are not all organised in academic year groups.

Perhaps staff from baby units could rotate with staff from over 3s and 'move up', with their key children, maintaining the attachments and relationships they have already built with the children from the start. This would obviously only work within the same setting and it may not work easily for qualified teaching staff or for those not experienced with babies. There have also been training and staffing implications and this has not been straightforward.

To support the children progressing from the under 3s to the over 3s in one of the settings, the children always joined the same group with the same Key Person. This Key Person works shifts and the children have become familiar with her because she sometimes works with the additional hours children in the under-3s building. She also runs a holiday club in the school holidays and all the children begin to get to know her then.

How many is too many?

Where I have been part of a very large overall staff group, with some staff working part-time, continuity of relationships can be much more difficult to maintain. A large number of staff can dilute the effectiveness of the relationship with the key attachment figure that is essential for these very young children. Sometimes, there seems to have been confusion and lack of unity amongst staff about how to relate to the children. If a child needs comfort and nurturing they need a key attachment figure they know well. If a child needs behavioural boundaries they need a key figure with a consistent approach to behaviour management who knows them well. In both cases, children need the security that can be provided by one or maybe two Key Persons. They may be confused by too many different approaches and ways of relating by professionals who don't know them so well.

Ensuring a consistency of approach has sometimes been a real challenge. One very positive aspect of one setting was the consistency of the staff team. There were not frequent changes of staff but there were many students who had short-term and longer-term placements and they needed time to adjust and support in adopting the setting's different strategies.

What has really made a difference in my experience is the existence of a second Key Person. When part-time staff are absent (or any staff due to sickness) the second or co-Key Person is consistently able to step in to replace the Key Person, thus reducing the number of attachment figures for the children to bond with. Both Key Persons are then able to provide nurturing relationships and security. They support particular children at particular times and know the children well.

Parents' feelings

Developing significant relationships between parents and young children is key to their learning and development. Occasionally staff may hold back for fear that parents will object to adults other than themselves getting close to their child, getting to know their children well or even, in some rare cases, better than they do. I have found this to happen only rarely but some practitioners are more cautious than others.

It is important to work with parents and to help them understand the way settings work. To take this forward, sometimes, it has been possible to offer training sessions to parents on topics like attachment and child development.

Communicating and not communicating

In multicultural, multi-lingual settings, the range of languages and cultures can make it more challenging for the Key Person to form good relationships with all the children in their group. It has really made a difference when there have been bilingual support staff. But then it has been essential that Key People make sure they speak to the bilingual staff to find out as much as they can about the children. Some settings created booklets written in the main languages that the Key Persons could take on home visits. These contained information and photos about the nursery, for the child to see before they start.

In one setting, a simple child-friendly leaflet written in English was devised for all the children to keep. It included the name of the Key Person and group the child would be in as well as drawings, photographs and other information, about coming to nursery. The family had something to share and to keep about nursery in the first few weeks.

When bilingual support staff were matched with children for the language spoken at home, they can speak to the child or parent and can translate for the Key Person if necessary. When these children start nursery, the bilingual staff member that went to the home then continued the relationship with that child and their family and is someone they could understand. I have even observed some of these staff members using their own time to support families dealing with difficult situations outside the nursery, such as hospital or housing issues. They try to be available at other times to help the child settle by speaking in their own language and supporting the parents and families when the child starts nursery.

But it is important for bilingual support staff to translate carefully any significant observations for the Key Person showing progress if necessary, especially in areas of personal, social and emotional development. They are encouraged to model the English language as well as using the home tongue when working alongside children with English as an additional language to help them pick up the English. This also helps children develop relationships with their English speaking Key Person.

It has been important too that the Key Person takes responsibility for talking regularly to the support staff about their shared children so that they are aware of what is being spoken about. Times for conversations like this are difficult to find, especially when staff work part time or shifts. As much as possible the two members of staff would work as a team to support the children and their family together.

But I miss you!

In the larger settings where children have had many different staff relating to them and dealing with the families, it can be confusing for the children. Different people have different tones of voice, a different manner and way of relating and different ways of dealing with things. Some children have asked for or looked for their Key Person when they are absent and pounce on them whenever they are there! Children do seem able to show that they need the security of knowing who is going to be there for them and they often want their Key Person whenever possible. They miss them when they are not there. Even when children do not really seem to mind, I would argue that they too need the security and continuity of a Key Person.

Group time squeezed

The time the Key Person has with their children together as a group has often seemed very limited. It is usually at the end of each session so as not to break into children's play. It can be rather rushed, just before the parents arrive to collect the children.

Staff have often had differing views about what the 'group time' is for. Is group time a social time or an opportunity for teaching the whole group or just a time for a story? Staff have had different ideas because they have had different experience, training and views about how best to use that time. A few years ago the children were older in the nursery settings. Now they are younger and many find it hard to focus for any length of time. This is another factor affecting time spent with key groups.

Big open-plan spaces do not always seem helpful regarding contact with Key

Person children. Nurseries with a number of rooms to divide the space have a different atmosphere and staff may encounter children in different ways in these differing environments.

When staff rotate between different learning environments the children they encounter are usually determined by the children's activity preferences. A Key Person may not see some of their children from one week to the next because they are not choosing to play in the area they are working.

However, some settings found that children who were very dependent on their Key Person actually follow the Key Person around into the spaces they are working. The positive side of this is that a child who may never go outside normally, will be exposed to a new and different experience. Once a child is not so reliant on the Key Person, it is positive that they are able to independently pick and choose where they wish to spend their time.

When settings placed more importance on regular training, or at least discussion about group times, this did help clarify the purpose and consistency between groups. Issues related to consistency and equal opportunities for teaching and learning for all children could then be aired and discussed. Questions like the opportunities for rich learning experiences and whether attachments are being strengthened could be looked at in more depth.

Keeping fully briefed

It was often difficult to plan times to discuss observations with each practitioner interacting with children, especially in the absence of the Key Person. Part-time/job-sharing staff rarely get a chance to meet each other and they relied on speaking on the phone to have these important conversations. We have wondered about how to plan in routine liaisons at a set part of the week or even every day. Ideally the Key Person and their co-Key Person meet regularly to talk about the children, share ideas, information, observations about what the children have been doing and to discuss things like organisation, future planning and so on, based on the child's needs and interests.

The Key Person's role and settling in

In most settings the older children usually start nursery at the start of the year and there is a staggered entry maybe up to around half term when the youngest start. The Key Person needs to be one who is there to greet them on the open day and then on their first day. They can talk to the parents, show them round, etc., and this is a continuation of the relationship begun at the home visit. But as mentioned earlier, this is tricky to administer. Often the starting dates are difficult to match with part-time staff's hours. Sometimes more than one or two children in a Key Person's group are starting on the same day, meaning the Key Person's attention is divided, and so on. Ideally, the Key Person should not have new children starting on consecutive days in case a child needs more support on day 2 or when the parents leave them for the first time.

If Key People had a direct part in the allocation of children to groups and the administration and organisation of children's starting dates and home visits, it is more likely that children can be matched to Key People at crucial times.

It could, however, in a large setting, mean it takes a long time for all the children to start. If the co-Key Person helped with the process, twice the number of children could start each day and meet their two Key Persons. I know this is very difficult to administer and very often parents change from morning to afternoon sessions, move in and out of the area, change their minds or do not even tell the setting what their plans are.

The importance these issues are given determines how much thought, planning and time goes into working all this out. It is complicated and more difficult and would take up a lot more administration time than a system based on children starting nursery in age order, but it is not impossible.

The role of record-keeping

In most of the settings each Key Person is responsible for gathering evidence in the form of observations, photographs, drawings and field notes for their group. These are the main sources of information drawn on for compiling profiles on each child. All staff make observations of all the children they are working with, which they share with each other regularly.

It is not always easy if the Key Person is not seeing some children as much as others. They rely on observations from other staff but the context of these is not always clear. Ideally, staff explain the observations they have made and try to put them into a context for the Key Person if they weren't present.

Record-keeping in the form of profiles is a great way to build up a picture of each child's development and progress in a readable and accessible way. Most settings find there is little time to discuss observations with colleagues. These times during a normal nursery day are limited and often rushed. Maybe this should become part of the timetable.

Extending Key Persons practice through reception and Key Stage 1

When children move on to infant or primary school, there is not always a shared understanding about the Key Persons approach and little opportunity for key staff to support children in the transition to school. Some of the settings have good liaison and well-planned transitions, others find this more difficult and communication with the next classes is limited.

It seems important, wherever possible, to take children to visit new schools before they start and to visit them once they have started. This depends on the cooperation of the school. Some settings have worked hard to gain closer links with local schools so that they can develop this aspect of the Key Person's role, although this requires a lot of time and planning and is not easy.

References

Adamo, S. (2001) '"The house is a boat": The experience of separation in a nursery school', *The International Journal of Infant Observation*, 4 (2): 135–6.

Alexander, R. (ed.) (2009) *Children, Their World, Their Education: Final report and recommendations of the Cambridge Primary Review*, London: Routledge. (Also interim press release published 2007, University of Cambridge.)

Alvarez, A. (1992) *Live Company Psychoanalytic Psychotherapy with Autistic, Borderline, Deprived and Abused Children*, London: Routledge.

Arnold, C. (1999) *Child Development and Learning 2–5 years: Georgia's story*, London: Paul Chapman.

Arnold, C. (2003) *Observing Harry: Child development and learning 0–5 years*. Maidenhead, UK: Open University Press.

Arnold, C. (2009) 'Understanding "Together and Apart": A case study of Edward's explorations at nursery', *Early Years*, 29 (2), July: 119–30.

Athey, C. (2007) *Extending Thought in Young Children* (2nd edition), London: Paul Chapman.

Bain, A. and Barnett, L. (1986) *The Design of a Day Care System in a Nursery Setting for Children Under Five: An abridged version of a report of an action research project* (Document No. 2T347), Institute of Human Relations for the Department of Health and Social Security (1975–1979), London: Tavistock Institute of Human Relations.

Barn, R. (2010) Chair, Research Seminar, University of London, 19 April 2010, *Mothering across Racialised Boundaries: Interdisciplinary perspectives in a changing world* (publication forthcoming).

Barn, R. (forthcoming) Paper given at 2010 conference *Black Voices Network* led by Patrice Lawrence at the National Children's Bureau.

Barnes, J., Leach, P., Sylva, K., Stein, A., Malmberg, L.E. and the FCCC team (2006) 'Infant care in England: Mothers' aspirations, experiences, satisfaction and caregiver relationships', *Early Child Development and Care*, 176 (5): 553–73.

Bateman, A. (1998) 'Child protection, risk and allegation', in Owen, C., Cameron, C. and Moss, P. (eds) *Men as Workers in Services for Young Children: Issues of a mixed gender workforce*, Proceedings of a Seminar held at Henley on Thames, 29–31 May 1997, London: Institute of Education, University of London, pp. 182–9.

Belsky, J., Burchinal, M., McCartney, K., Vandell, D., Clarke-Stewart, K. and Owen, M.T. (2007) 'Are there long term effects of early child care?' *Child Development*, 78 (2): 681–701.

Bowlby, J. (1988) *A Secure Base: Clinical applications of attachment theory*, London: Routledge.

Brooker, L. (2002) *Starting School: Young children learning cultures*, Milton Keynes: Open University Press.

Brooks-Gunn. J., Sidle-Fuligni, A. and Berlin. L. J. (eds) (2003) *Early Child Development in the 21st Century: Profiles of Current Research Initiatives*. New York: Teachers College Press.

Cameron, C., Moss, P. and Owen, C. (1999) *Men in the Nursery: Gender and caring work*, London: Paul Chapman.

Connolly, P. (1998) *Racism, Gender, Initiatives and Young Children*, London: Routledge.

Dahlberg, G., Moss, P. and Pence, A. (1999) *Beyond Quality in Early Childhood Education and Care: Postmodern perspectives*, London: Falmer Press.

DCSF (Department for Children, Schools and Families) (2007a) *Local Authority Briefing Pack for the Early Years Foundation Stage, Part 2*, London: DCSF.

DCSF (2007b, revised 2008) *Practice Guidance for the Early Years Foundation Stage*, London: DCSF.

DCSF (2007c, revised 2008) *Statutory Framework for the Early Years Foundation Stage*, London: DCSF.

DCSF (2007d) *The Early Years Foundation Stage: Principles into practice*, London: DCSF.

Dennis, E. (2001) 'Seeing beneath the surface: An observer's encounter with a child's struggle to find herself at nursery', *International Journal of Infant Observation*, 4 (2): 107–120.

Dettling, A., Gunnar, M. and Donzella, B.l. (1999) 'Cortisol levels of young children in full day care centres', *Psychoneuroendocrinology*, 24: 519–36.

Dettling, A.C., Parker, S.W., Lane, S., Sebanc, A. and Gunnar, M.R. (2000) 'Quality of care and temperament determine changes in cortisol concentrations over the day for young children in childcare', *Psychoneuroendocrinology*, Vl (25): 819–836.

DfES (Department for Education and Skills) (2002) *Birth to Three Matters: A framework for supporting early years practitioners*, London: DfES SureStart Unit.

DfES (2004) *Effective Provision of PreSchool Education (EPPE) Project. Findings from Preschool to end of Key Stage 1*. Sylva, K., Melhuish, E., Sammons, P., Siraj-Blatchford, I. and Taggart, B. DfES (1997–2004). Report 18596.

DfES (2007) *The Early Years Foundation Stage*, London: DfES Publications.

Department of Health (1991) *The Children Act 1989 Guidance and Regulations, Volume 2: Family support, day care and educational provision for young children*, London: HMSO.

de Zulueta, F. (2001) Personal communication with authors.

Duffy, B. (2000) 'The Key Person in action at the Thomas Coram Early Excellence Centre', unpublished submission to Department for Education and Employment, October.

Early Childhood Forum (ECF, formerly The Early Childhood Education Forum) (2006) *Strategy and Policy agenda 2006–9*. Available online at www.ncb.uk/ecf.

Elfer, P. (1996) 'Building intimacy in relationships with young children in nurseries', *Early Years*, 16 (2): 30–4.

Elfer, P. (2006) 'Exploring children's expressions of attachment in nursery', *European*

Journal of Early Childhood Education and Research, 14 (2): 81–95.

Elfer, P. (2008) '5000 hours: Organising for intimacy in the care of children under three attending full time nursery', unpublished Ph.D., University of East London.

Elfer, P. and Dearnley, K. (2007) 'Nurseries and emotional well-being: Evaluating an emotionally containing model of professional development', *Early Years: An International Journal of Research and Development*, 27 (3): 267–79.

Elfer, P. and Selleck, D. (1999) 'Children under three in nurseries: Uncertainty as a creative factor in child observations', *European Early Childhood Research Journal*, 7 (1): 69–82.

Every Child a Talker (2008) http://www.dcsf.gov.uk/pns/DisplayPN.cgi?pn_id=2008_0141

Geddes, H. (2006) *Attachment in the Classroom*, London: Worth Publications.

Gerhardt, S. (2004) *Why Love Matters: How affection shapes a baby's brain*, London: Brunner-Routledge.

Glover, L. and Glover, B. (2001) Personal communication with authors.

Goldschmied, E. and Jackson, S. (1994) *People Under Three: Young children in day care*, London: Routledge.

Goldschmied, E. and Jackson, S. (2004) *People Under Three: Young children in day care* (2nd edition), London: Routledge.

Goldschmied, E. and Selleck, D. (1996) *Communication between Babies in their First Year*, London: National Children's Bureau (booklet and video).

Greenfield, S. (forthcoming) *Journal of Early Childhood Research*.

Hay, S. (1996) *Special Issues in Nursery Management*, London: Baillière Tindall Ltd.

Hopkins, J. (1988) 'Facilitating the development of intimacy between nurses and infants in day nurseries', *Early Child Development and Care*, 33: 99–111.

Jackson, E. (2008) 'The development of work discussion groups in educational settings', *Journal of Child Psychotherapy*, 34 (1): 62–82.

Lane, J. (2008) *Young Children and Racial Justice: Taking action for racial equality in the early years – understanding the past, thinking about the present, planning for the future*, London: National Children's Bureau.

Lane, J. (2010) 'Institutional discrimination in the early years', *Race Equality Teaching*, 28 (3), Summer.

Lane, J. and Ouseley, H. (2010) *Review of the Early Years Foundation Stage: Focus on equality of opportunity*. Available from jane@janelane.plus.com.

Lawrence, P. (2010) *Speaking on behalf of the Black Childcare Network*, London: NCB. (See also Barn 2010.)

Leach, P. (2008) 'Relationships and feelings in the nursery', *Nursery World*, 6 November, pp. 21–8. Available online at http://www.nurseryworld.co.uk/news/login/859391/EYFS-best-practice-relationships-feelings-nursery/?DCMP=ILC-SEARCH

Leach, P. (2009) *Child Care Today: What we know and what we need to know*, Cambridge: Polity.

Leach, P., Barnes, J., Nichols, M., Goldin, J., Stein, A., Sylva, K., Malmberg, L.E. and the FCCC team (2006) 'Child care before 6 months of age: A qualitative study of mothers' decisions and feelings about employment and non-maternal care', *Infant and Child Development: An international journal of research*, 15 (5): 471–502.

Lestrange, M. (2010) 'Developing the Key Person approach in schools: Case studies from the Manchester Buddying Project', handouts at the Manchester Early Years Annual conference, 21 June 2010.

MacAndrew, J.C. (2010) 'Sam and his blanket', unpublished.

McCreery, E., Jones, L. and Holmes, R. (2007) 'Why do Muslim parents want Muslim schools?' *Early Years*, 27 (3), October: 203–19.

Manning-Morton, J. (2006) 'The personal is professional: Professionalism and the birth to three practitioner', *Contemporary Issues in Early Childhood*, 7 (1): 42–52.

Manning-Morton, J. and Thorp, M. (2001) *Key Times: A framework for developing high quality provision for children under three years old*, London: Camden Local Education Authority and University of North London.

Mathers, S., Sylva, K. and Joshi, H. with Hansen, K., Plewis, I., Johnson, J., George, A., Linskey, F. and Grabbe, Y. (2007) *Quality of Childcare Settings in the Millennium Cohort Study*. Department of Educational Studies, University of Oxford and Institute of Education, University of London. London: HMSO.

Melhuish, E. (2004) *Child Benefits: The importance of investing in quality childcare* (Facing the Future Policy Papers), London: Daycare Trust.

Miller, L. (1992) *Understanding Your Baby*, London: Rosendale Press.

Ministry of Health and Ministry of Education (1945, 14 December) *Nursery Provision for Children under Five* (Circular 221/45), London: HMSO.

Munn, P. and Schaffer, R. H. (1993) 'Literacy and Numeracy Events in Social Interactive Contexts', *International Journal of Early Years Education*, 1 (3): 61–80.

National Strategies (2009) 'Learning, playing and interacting in the early years foundation stage', London: DCSF.

National Strategies Early Years (2008) *The Social and Emotional Aspects of Development: Guidance for practitioners working in the Early Years Foundation Stage*, London: DCSF.

NICHD (National Institute of Child Health and Human Development Early Child Care Research Network) (1997) 'The effect of infant child care on infant–mother attachment security: Results of the NICHD Study of Early Child Care', *Child Development*, 68 (5): 860–79.

Nutbrown, C. and Page, J. (2008) *Working with Babies and Children: From Birth to Three*. London: Sage.

OECD (Organisation for Economic Co-operation and Development) (2005) *Babies and Bosses*, Paris: OECD.

Page, J. (2008) 'Permission to love them but not too much', in Nutbrown, C. and Page, J., *Working with Babies and Children: From birth to three*, London: Sage, pp. 181–7.

Pugh, G and Sylva, K (2005) Transforming the early years in England. *Oxford Review of Education*, Vol 31, Number 1, March 2005, pp. 11–27(17).

Randolph Beresford Centre (1999) 'Unpublished working notes: The Key Person approach in practice'. London Borough of Hammersmith and Fulham.

Raikes, H. (1996) 'A secure base for babies: Applying attachment concepts to the infant care setting', *Young Children*, 51 (5): 59–67.

Read, V. (2010) *Developing Attachment in Early Years Settings: Nurturing secure relationships from birth to five*, Abingdon: Routledge.

Roberts, R. (2005) *Resilient Well Being Project*, action research with Oxfordshire County Council, EYDCP, and Sure Start (leaflet).

Roberts, R. (2010) *Well Being from Birth*, London: Sage.

Roberts-Holmes, G. (2004) '"I am a little bit brown and a little bit white": A dual heritage young boy's playful identity construction', *Race Equality Teaching*, 23 (1): 15–20.

Robinson, M. (2003) 'From birth to one: The year of opportunity', in *The Personal in the Professional*, Milton Keynes: Open University Press.

Robinson, M. (2011) *Understanding Behaviour and Development in Early Childhood*, Abingdon: Routledge.

Rogoff, B. (2003) *The Cultural Nature of Human Development*, Oxford and New York: Oxford University Press.

Rustin, M. (1989) 'Introduction', in Miller, L., Rustin, M.E., Rustin, M.J. and Shuttleworth, J. (eds), *Closely Observed Infants*, London: Duckworth.

Rutter, M. (2002) 'Nature, nurture and development: From evangelism, through science towards policy and practice', *Child Development*, 73 (1): 1–21.

Schaffer, H.R. (1998) *Making Decisions About Children: Psychological questions and answers*, Oxford: Blackwell.

Schore, R. (1997) *Rethinking the Brain: New Insights into Early Development*. New York: Families and Work Institute.

Selleck, D.Y. (2006a) 'Being included: Being "brown", being me! Beginning at the beginning', in *Race Equality Teaching*, 24 (2): 33–38.

Selleck, D.Y. (2006b) 'Key persons in the early years foundation stage', *Early Education*, 50: 11–13.

Selleck, D.Y. (2009) 'The Key Persons approach in reception classes in early education', *Early Education*, 57: 3–5.

Selleck, D.Y. (2010) '"Key Group Time" is a time for intimacy. "Circle time" is a time for group thinking. Why they must be different', *Early Childhood Practice: The Journal for Multi-professional Partnerships*, 11, (1&2): 124–30.

Shields, P. (2009) '"School doesn't feel much of a partnership": Parents' perceptions of their children's transition from nursery school to reception class', *Early Years Journal*, 9 (3): 237–48.

Shore, R. (1997) *Rethinking the Brain: New insights into early development*, New York: Families and Work Institute.

Shropshire and Telford and Wrekin Early Years and Child Care Development Partnership (2000) 'Joint training initiative: Staff development for baby and toddler observations in group care'. LEA internal publication, January.

Siraj-Blatchford, I. and Manni, L. (2008) '"Would you like to tidy up now?" An analysis of adult questioning in the English Foundation Stage', *Early Years*, 28 (1): 5–22.

Slatter, B. (2005) *What We Think About Starting School* and *Social and Emotional Aspects of Development*, Oxford: Oxfordshire County Council and EYDCP and Sure Start.

Syal, M. (1997) *Anita and Me*, London: Flamingo.

Trevarthen, C. (1994) *An Infant in the Family: Developing knowledge with personality*,

Edinburgh: The British Psychological Society, Scottish Branch.

Trevarthen, C. (1999) from a recorded interview for BBC Radio 4; and in Purvis, L. and Selleck, D., *Tuning in to Children*, London: BBC Education.

Tronick, E. (2005) 'Why is connection with others so critical? The formation of dyadic states of consciousness and the expansion of individuals' states of consciousness: Coherence governed selection and the co-creation of meaning out of messy meaning making', in Nadel, J. and Muir, D. (eds), *Emotional Development*, Oxford: Oxford University Press, pp. 293–315.

Watson, H. (2002) 'Report on practice at the Netherton Park Family Centre', National Children's Homes Action for Children. Personal communication with authors.

Whalley, M. (1996) 'Working as a team', in Pugh, G. (ed.), *Contemporary Issues in the Early Years: Working collaboratively for children* (2nd edition), London: Paul Chapman Publishing, pp. 170–88.

Index